GULLERS STOCKHOLM

View of Björkö (Birch Island) in Mälar Lake, where an important market served much of what is now Northern Europe and parts of Russia for nearly 300 years until the late 11th century.

Botkyrka church, from the 12th century.

Essingeleden, the main north-south traffic route through Stockholm.

STOCK

Photographs: Peter Gullers and others
Designed by Lasse Hallbert
Published by Gullers Pictorial AB, Stockholm

6

HOLM

Strindberg's view from Mosebacke described in The Red Room *has been obscured by a large office building: this bit of photographic magic has re-created it.*

THE SOUNDS OF STOCKHOLM

By Oscar Hedlund

A town is more than its houses and streets and vehicles and people, it's all of them and their sounds together.

Once, in a radio competition, Stockholm's premiere sound was to be chosen, and suggestions flooded in: the chimes of City Hall; the alarm at Central Station; *tunnelbana* echoes; clogs clattering along Västerlånggatan in the Old City; stamping of boots on guard at Slottsbacken; Waxholm steamers' and Djurgård ferries' wakes slopping against quays; seagulls' skrieks and street sellers' calls; stallkeepers crying their wares on Saturdays in Hötorget — but no-one was surprised when Stadshuset's chimes won.

A good second, however, was bird song in Humlegården, against a mild traffic hum from Stureplan. It's all so long ago now. Only the alarm remains, its indefinite, thick doughy sound hardly suggesting poetry.

Who sings nowadays of traffic hum? What music's in heavy sighs of ventilation fans, in jagged fragments of noise from freestyles, in yelps from car and burglar alarms, or thumps from rock-blasting portables, or traffic-signal clicks, or hoarse roars of burners under hot-air balloons, or tinkles from Americanised ice-cream trucks?

Sounds echo the town's constant change, rising, falling, and dying away. They're often remarked only when absent, but lend an ear now, and listen to Stockholm!

Bellman* did, in the ecstatic collage of sound in Epistle 33, *On Father Mowitz' Crossing to Djurgården,* and so did Strindberg, most famously in the first chapter of *The Red Room:*

Far beneath him the newly-woken town rumbled and clattered: steam winches spun on the quays, pigs of iron tumbled on the scales, lock-keepers shrilled their whistles, vessels along Skeppsbron blew off steam, busses from Kungsback battered and jumped over the cobbles, fishwives and seagulls shrieked by the stalls, sails and flags shook and flapped out on the waters of Strömmen, horns signalled from Skeppsholmen, drill-sergents bawled from Södermalmstorg, workers' clogs rattled along Glasbruksgatan — all made an impression of life and movement . . .

That celebrated earful from the terrace at Mosebacke is stereophonically clear, calling up sounds Stockholm lacks today. They may not have been so strong, but they must have been distinct and clear.

9

Two worldmasters of sound from Stockholm: Eric Ericson as choir-master, and Georg Bolin with his guitars. What unites their disciplines is their abilities to make sounds clear, to cause their tones to sparkle like the finest Swedish crystal.

"And above all, they varied, on a gliding scale from soft to thunderous," says Professor Georg Bolin, who has his world-famous guitar studio on the heights of the South Side, where the carpet of sound from the town drapes itself over his acoustic instruments.

"What makes sound like town noise a plague is its monotony; its machine-like regularity as it were clogs our ears with its lack of contrasts or tensions between strong and weak frequencies. Just an indistinguishable mumble, an anonymous rumble, from the traffic machine, but more than anything else, from ventilation fans. They're the worst."

Georg Bolin believes our senses are dulled most by the lack of contrast in town noise.

"While I may be elderly, I never knew Strindberg's time but I'm prepared to bet sounds varied more then: between different seasons and times of day, between Sundays and working days. Sounds on a summer evening differ essentially from sounds in a snow-covered landscape . . . and one's always re-making the discovery of how sound so easily on a windstill day carries over water — everything seems to be enlarged, closer. It's simply because there's no resistance, sound waves can move freely against the most reinforcing background there is for sound: silence. Today silence is something

more and more rarely encountered. Fragments of sounds like layers of acoustic dust fill every crack and pore of the town."

Bolin sometimes enlivens his lectures with his lighthouse-keeper story.

"A lighthouse keeper lived alone on his remote station, its silence broken every half minute by a cannon shot that served as an acoustic signal. Year in and year out the same thunderous sound, every thirty seconds . . . until one night the cannon failed to work. A prolonged silence followed. The lighthouse keeper fell out of his bunk with the frightened cry: "Who the devil fired?!""

Georg Bolin believes a jumble of sound is more dulling for the ears.

"We don't notice it because it's never silent and now, for example, ornithologists know bird song is rare in inner Stockholm, and we can hardly hear seagulls and terns. Big-city dwellers' supposed characteristic is not responding to sounds — not even to the most lovely sound I know in Stockholm: water clucking and rustling everywhere in cracks between rocks and sounding precisely as it really is — clean!" Bolin says you can still hear this sometimes, but you have to hold your breath and lean down almost to the water.

Someone else who lends an ear is the music writer, Ludvig Rasmusson*, who first listened and then wrote his piece "The music of cities in the future."

The rhythm of the seasons and daily rhythms have their basic sounds: "The New Year begins with the pealing of bells. We open windows and the chill of the winter night streams in. It's quite quiet, for no-one drives a car just when the new year begins. The few taxis on the streets drive up to telephone booths, drivers get out to ring friends and wish them a happy new year. Rockets have been heard all the evening, but their whistling and banging is smothered by the bells. We never hear peals like those during the first seconds of a new year.

"It's a beautiful and promising prelude to a new year of sound over the town.

"In January snow muffles sounds. Snow ploughs and other machines roar, cars slither and, on roofs, snow clearers scramble about and call to one another in Finnish. No month has less bird song than January, and February is hardly better. In March ice and packed snow begins to thaw and drip by day. Some birds return: sparrows chirp in bushes.

"By April streets are free of ice and snow, and once again one can hear at a distance high-heeled shoes on pavements. Children in back-yards call and shout. Migrant birds return, bicycles squeak.

"In May and June bird-song culminates, and blackbirds sing long into the night. Trees in full leaf stifle the noise of traffic, their crowns sigh in the wind. It rains, soon followed by thunder. May Day demonstrations troop through the town. Street musicians can be heard again. In Stockholm, the peak of the sounds of the year is the six-week period between Walpurgis Night and end of school term in early June.

"Later, things are quieter, and during July traffic is at its quietest. But indoors one can hear all sounds clearly, for one opens the windows on account of the heat. Ventilation fans are never heard so clearly, and by August traffic noise begins to increase again.

"Then the birds begin to sing again. One hears migrating birds, leaves rustle underfoot, and November winds whine and howl in naked branches. Street musicians retreat into *tunnelbana* entries. Eagle owls hoot in their cages on Skansen.

Canvas snapping in the wind, the heathen sounds of tackle and rigging . . . sounds heard now only when events such as the Tall Ships' Race occur.

(Top left) Electric guitars and clashing cymbals in Kungsträdgården mix with the swish from kids on slides. (Above) But from Sergelstorg, at the heart of the town, all that is to be heard is the melancholy silence of a mime artist.

And at distant Skeppsholmen jazz fans honour visiting world celebrities with rattles of applause, while the reek of grilled sausages and kebabs glitters against the light.

The numbers of guards on duty at the palace diminish and eventually only a single drummer marches and ruffles in the cold. By Christmas it's quite quiet, and church bells begin to ring again . . . "

Rasmusson's kaleidoscope of Stockholm sounds has become a classic, but I believe the idea of Stockholm and sound is linked to the town's entertainment life: rock, jazz, community singing in parks, street musicians, musical shows, organ music seeping out of half-open church doors in summer, open-air concerts, jazz pubs, pianos in bars . . .

Particularly in summer, Stockholm's become one of the most densely entertained towns in the world, even if we can't yet compete with New York, where there're said to be on average 400 music events every evening. But here things are closer together, so to say.

Mats Liljefors* is now a permanent fixture of Stockholm in summer. When he began his summer concerts *Musik på slottet* in the palace in Stockholm sixteen years ago he was just about alone.

15

"The Stockholm Festival had come to an end because the authorities with the purse strings got it into their heads that music was nothing for a town in summer . . . who would want to sit and listen to a concert on a summer evening?"

Stockholm has always been keen on amusements, perhaps because of our Lutheran inheritance, our need to ease the burden of the awful grey blanket at any price, which is what it usually costs.

As early as the thirteenth century, Snorri Sturluson* had his suspicions: in his *Ynglingasagan** the bard describes the horrid end awaiting those who laugh and snigger at "the sort of dreadful rubbish wandering hoarse-voiced beggars strew about in the streets."

So from the start, Stockholm's nightlife has had the forbidden, shameful atmosphere that comes from "vulgarities." Not unexpectedly the church was first in the field to keep an eye on public order. Long into the fifteenth century, amongst the worst of enjoyments was choir song, of all things! The church was disturbed when choir song sounded altogether too beautiful, lest it lure the congregation to listen more to the music than to the priest speaking of the damnation awaiting sinners.

"The pope had the final word as to whether those heathen in the north — that's to say, the Swedes — might be permitted to sing in their churches," explained Eric Ericsson, Professor of Choir Song at Stockholm University. After nearly a half century of working with choirs from all over the world he if anyone knows how lovely a choir can sound.

"It took choristers centuries of cunning to get past the ears of a severe clergy, and to sing out all the heavenly beauty and happiness music can bring with it . . . but of course it was profane pleasure in the midst of serious religion."

Those heathen up there in the north, on their scarcely entertaining tundra, have never needed much encouragement to indulge in fun and merriment. Stockholm's guide to nightlife extends, in fact, just about to the start of the town.

If the Albert Hall is the best-known venue for proms, the prom outside the Maritime Museum in Stockholm by the Stockholm Philharmonic attracts about 30,000 people every August.

Antal Dorati conducts the Stockholm Philharmonic in Beethoven's Missa Solemnis. The organ is from 1982, and was built by the Swedish firm of Grönlunds.

One of the many non-musical events at the Hall: a meeting of the Swedish Forestry Association.

A quite ordinary day at the Concert Hall

A monumental 1920s' building, the Stockholm Concert Hall was designed by Ivar Tengbom* and embellished with work by leading contemporary Swedish artists, among them Isaac Grünewald*. Its colonnaded western facade, enlivened with the Orpheus fountain by Milles*, forms one side of the Hötorget marketplace.

The Hall is host to many events, of which the Nobel prize awards must be the best known. It has been at the centre of Stockholm's music life, for example, since it was built for the Stockholm Philharmonic, now nearing its seventy-fifth birthday, and now a leading international orchestra.

In spring 1987, after playing in Spain, it was rehearsing Arne Mellnäs* Ikaros Symphony for its first public performance, before leaving for Austria, Czechoslovakia, the German Democratic Republic, and Yugoslavia. Paavo Berglund* had just succeeded Yuri Ahronovitch, its leader since 1982. In addition to its many tours, it records regularly, a recent disc being Shostakovitch' Fifth Symphony.

In summer, it plays in open-air concerts arranged together with *Dagens Nyheter*, the Stockholm daily, and the city's parks' administration. Its members enjoy close contact with the rest of Stockholm's music life — final-year students at the Stockholm College of Music hold graduation concerts at the Hall, and many chamber-music and other groups rehearse and perform there. Musicologists from all over the world meet in its library or in its information department.

The annual Nobel prize awards are not the only royal events at the Hall. HM King Carl Gustaf and HM Queen Silvia graced the 1987 congress of the Swedish Forestry Association with their presence and presented medallions to distinguished members.

With so much varied activity at the Concert Hall, it's impossible to say if a day's events are 'typical,' but they're always a rewarding experience.

A working day at the Hall: repetitions, meetings, and more repetitions.

SWINGING STOCKHOLM

By Oscar Hedlund

By the turn of the century, Bern's was the 40 year-old centre of Stockholm pleasure life, and famed as Strindberg's Red Room.

Christina*, a real Queen of Pleasure, reigned in Sweden then, and at her court it was not done to mention the cost of entertainments – the country was to fortify her great-power status after the successful wars, her flaxen-haired farmers were to be inducted into continental habits, and the Queen had commanded the presence of the best of what Europe could offer in the way of dancers, clowns and musicians.

To celebrate her twenty-fifth birthday, she permitted herself to be regaled by, among other things, a ballet costing one hundred thousand *thalers*. A sour footnote to the exchequer accounts for 1652–53 records that in less than ten years the queen "had thrown away 13,174,950 over and above the usual incomes of the Realm, which has caused the Realm real losses of Capital."

Before her majesty tired of it and left for Rome, she had made Stockholm swing a little. A high-life whirlpool of courtly and other grandees, and some members of the bourgeoisie, sucked even "common residents of the town" into such awful delights as tilting at a ring at the Tiltyard, near Hötorget, "with real Turks."

One of the more persistent sounds of eighteenth-century Stockholm was the shuffle and click of cards. Perhaps not disapproved of if indulged in in the right sort of privacy, "gaming, dicing and wagering for money in streets, squares, alleys, harbours" were all prohibited, in an attempt to abate the "flow of noise in churchyards, both during and between services." Shady gambling clubs of our day – or, rather, night – can thus claim they maintain an historical tradition when police shake the bars on the doors and try to get in and raid the place.

Beerhalls and coffee houses were soon centres of entertainment in the town. *Brännvin* ran in streams during the eighteenth century – it was weaker then, so one drank even more of it. Bellman's songs and epistles are really eighteenth-century social workers' reports, with child deaths, plague and drunkenness noted along with bouts of fisticuffs, seduction and other elegeic pleasures, not forgetting semi-suicidal melancholy.

The pleasures of the town culminated some seventy years later, when the German confectioner Henrik Robert Bern opened his rooms by Berzelii Park, and so provided the gilded youth of Stockholm with its most popular meeting point. Light musical entertainment acquired a foothold that later sheltered what Swedes call variety – music-hall or burlesque entertainment, perhaps – from which developed the revue theatres of later years.

Our entertainment life has had its social aspects, for it's been a vital part of the changes of the nineteenth century. Under the influence of industrial development, everything that could be called 'entertainment' expanded. In addition, choir singing, now perhaps the most vital of all popular movements in Sweden, excepting only sport, could divert people from drowning themselves in cheap spirits. Virtually compulsory internal immigration to towns had led to miserable urban living conditions – of course people had to be gathered around something that cost nothing – song! Let them get together, let them sing! The teetotal and free-church movements thus became the foremost proponents of choir song.

During these decades Stockholm acquired a number of popular places of entertainment, from Bavarian beer halls to the Grand Hotel and the Opera Cellar Bar, which was envisaged first as a place for popular gatherings that would include "even the military and indeed, even diplomatists," as August Blanche* could state contentedly.

The really refined would never go near Mosebacke, where dances were conducted under the eye of fully-equipped police – sabres were standard equipment until the 1960s – and where fights on the floor would be extinguished by chucking all parties down into a cellar of soldiers who were moonlighting as a punishment squad.

Now the Inner-most of all In-places, the Opera Cellar had been planned as a place of mere popular resort.

Prohibition in one form or another has always stimulated the entertainment world. Jazz was born in Sweden in such an atmosphere, where the respectable bourgeoisie blocked their ears against "nigger howls." The Cecil, opened in 1917 as a restaurant, became the gathering point for the jazz boys of the town. According to the incomparable Karl Gerhard*, their trouser creases were characteristically "as sharp as a razor's edge."

Even old-style dance and accordion music has been enlivened by resistance to threats of prohibition. The Church of Sweden feared even breathless pauses between dances, if spent in loggias or on folding benches, would lead to widespread bastardy, for was not the violin the devil's own instrument? The accordion, however, being a favourite among farm hands and workers, was nothing for polite society, in which, on the other hand, it was quite the thing to succeed in cabare or revue. Never mind its origins in knockabout rural farce — bondkomik for farmers and clodhoppers would be transformed by Emil Norlander*, Sigge Wulff*, Jean Claeson*, Kalle Nämdeman*, Ernst Rolf* and the others.

Dance halls had their golden days between the wars, but in the 1940s jazz "poisoned the cream of the Swedish youth," to cite the Swedish Church's enquiry 'The Entertainment Habits of the Swedish Youth' (1941). Lurking 'dancehall evils' were first detected then, signs of the moral degeneration against which the Swedish youth of the time had to be protected. Their grandchildren today are perhaps as threatened by free-styles, videos and drugs, dangers no less terrible than those of the early 1940s: weekly magazines in colour, American films, modern music, but worse than all else, dance.

So dance halls and saloons sprang up like proverbial mushrooms, and thrived. The worst and rottenest of the lot, a place of fights and disorder called 'The National' (being shortened from Nationalen to Nalen) came into the care of a former Olympic medallist in hop, skip and jump, Gustaf Lindblom, nicknamed Topsy. In his hands, this agreeable sink of boxing, dancing, bicycle competitions and unlimited punch drinking became the centre of Swedish jazz for nearly forty years.

Latter-day sociologists have laid wreaths on Nalen's grave, for Topsy was everything a youth leader should be, a severe but teddy-bear-like father-figure for generations of Nalen-snajdare, as the dancers were called. Just as numerous, orthodox jazz fans stood like statues in front of the stage, lapping up the music, immoveable for hours, and God help anyone of them who was moved to dance!

A youth cult bloomed, although no-one would have called it that, and dance halls in general and Nalen in particular were at its centre. That extraordinary vitality and today's mechanised disco dunk-dunk differ in their music: the one live, the other ready-made.

Jazz and dance were so infectiously popular that the state consulted some of its doctors. They pursed their lips, and pronounced on the mental state of the young, and an appropriate remedy: "the eight-hour day is unsuitable for youth, it needs occupation for 15 to 16 hours lest it be led into idleness and loitering. The artifical legalised idleness in the form of over-reduced working hours seems to form the solid basis for the modern entertainment industry." Contemporary demands in the late 1980s, that over-demonstrative youth should be compulsorily enlisted in work battalions, aren't without precedent.

Anyway, our town, which Per Rådström* has called "a better sort of fishing harbour," dances as best it can, but no-one can deny that it has acquired more sounds, more addictions, more ambitions. Sure, restaurants have become more fun and one knows why: immigrants did not forget their own food and sense for independent service when they moved to Sweden — they've given the whole entertainment industry a boost it badly needed. There's much more money in the business, and much higher profits than in the days of the simple old halls, and the front money has to be much higher, too. Unfortunately, the range is narrower, there's less variety, things are "trend-conscious," and people in the business play a nervous unimaginative follow-my-leader game, where one success must be followed by another of the same sort, and everyone rushes in the same direction.

A sign of health are the local small restaurants and their half-amateur scenes. This is where the next generations' Povel Ramel*, Lill Lindfors*, Gösta Ekman*, Hasseåtage*, Monica Z*, Cornelis Vreeswijk*, Sten-Åke Cederhök*, Alice Babs* are going to be born.

Every sort of sound, every sort of crazy creator, must of course still be present in this wonderful town.

Nalen may be physically gone, now, but memories of 1960s twists keep stirring in some Stockholmers minds.

Stockholm is no museum of pleasures for the nostalgic, for its range of entertainments is wide and wild — from light opera at Oscars Theatre (left) to jazz at Stampen (below), and to a glittering pearly necklace of diskoteques and other places to dance in.

(Right) Discos have come far from the record libraries or record-shops in which they grew in the 1960s: handball is usually played in this disco-for-a-night, with its cascades of lights and all-enveloping sound, in which dancers move like the professionals (below right) in the Stockholm production of Cats.

Café Opera ranks as the Nr. 1 place in Stockholm, and at midnight it's the source of the liveliest noise in the Opera building. By daylight, with light reflected off the water of Strömmen outside, guests can admire what is perhaps the most beautiful restaurant ceiling in the world.

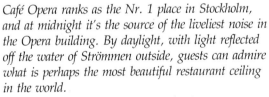

'Steamboat Beef,' or Ångbåtsbiff, isn't what it ought to be unless eaten on a steamer, a seeming truism that can be put to the test, nowadays, even during winter on skerries' ferries sailing from central Stockholm.

Thanks to immigrants, Stockholm has become an international eating town, with luxurious 'in' restaurants for traditional Swedish meals — husmanskost — to every sort of exotic speciality, from one end of Asia to the other.

This is Sollentuna, one of a score of golf clubs in the Stockholm region.

City Hall chimes ring out daily at noon in a melody named for St. George — Örjan is one of the Swedish versions of the name; here, towards sunset, a whining clump of cyclists lead what may be one of those lemming-like mass events towards the finishing line.

Running for straightforward pleasure through birdsong in an unhurried park or less obviously pleasurably over wet asphalt in a finishing spurt, cheered on by umbrella-shielded spectators.

The Baltic skerries outside Stockholm are a summer paradise.

The Old Town, with the curvy U-shape formed by — naturally — Western and Eastern long streets, Västerlånggatan och Österlånggatan.

A piece of medieval Stockholm lies under the immediate precincts of the renovated riksdagshus.

The medieval city neatly blocked the exit to the Baltic from the inland waterways of Mälaren.

ON HISTORICAL STOCKHOLM

By Lars Widding

Stockholm, a large modern city interspersed with much water, is full of traces of a dramatic past that, for me, was at its most dramatic during the eighteenth and early nineteenth centuries.

What do those conspiratorial masked young aristocrats have in mind as they make their various ways to a ball at the Opera on a gloomy March evening in 1792? A shot soon to echo from the stage will change the course of Swedish history — and in time will be commemorated in Verdi's *Un ballo in maschera*.

And senior officers hurrying at dawn on a winter's day up to the Palace in the Old Town: what revolutionary plans do they have? In an hour their king will flee across the inner court to rouse his guards — but will he be in time, or find the relief he seeks?

Such drama can well come to mind in central Stockholm, for if the actors in these dramas have long since found their graves, amazingly much of the Stockholm they knew has survived the enormous waves of construction that have swept across the city in the last few decades.

Stroll across to Riddarhuset in the Old Town: here, right in sight of this palatial building, an earl marshall of Sweden was butchered by the mob, under the noses of a troop of soldiers parading with loaded weapons, all on a summer's day in 1810!

And out across Strömmen, between the green of Kastellholmen and the heights of the South Side, a little puff of southerly wind caught *Wasa*'s few sails and hove her down; and she sank in the sunlight of an August day in 1628.

Least disturbed by recent changes is the Old Town, with its heart still in Stortorget, close to the German church and a stone's throw from the Palace. This stone-set square once ran with blood in the foulest bloodbath of Swedish history. A Dane who became king of Sweden in 1520 lured a hundred or more of his Swedish opponents into his power and on the pretext of a charge of heresy put them to the sword in this very square.

Neighbourly animosities persisted for a couple of centuries or more, but before long Stockholm was to reel under the onslaught of something even worse than Danes. The plague of 1710 took perhaps a third or even a half of Stockholm's population of some 40,000 in the course of its five or six months' rage. As graveyards were filled and over-filled, empty houses and tenements stood in dismal, plundered rows.

Yet a couple of generations later the town had recovered its strength, with a population half as large again as before the plague. To judge from the work of contemporary artists — Elias Martin, perhaps, more than any — the town might seem to have been a glittering idyll, its impressive stone-built mansions spreading along the shores of the central holms and islands, among timber-built houses and plain hovels. In fact, behind magnificent facades, mid-eighteenth-century Stockholm was a town of slums and hungry needy masses, with the highest child mortality of all cities in Europe.

The town, and especially its low life, was hymned by Carl Michael Bellman, who called it a "proud city;" one of his most celebrated epistles is set by Roddertrappan — the Rowers' Stairs — and on the waters of Strömmen below Slottsbacken, where the statue of Gustav III by *Sergel** stands today. Bellman's noisy boisterous burlesque company embarked for Djurgården, a few hundred metres across the water of the harbour; it was an international port then, and German and Dutch might be heard almost as often as Swedish.

Bellman also celebrated his monarch, Gustav

Stortorget, the Great Square, of the Old Town.

III — "the finest King of all who ruled the North." The poet worked actively in the royal public-relations campaign, for Gustav had made himself effectively sole ruler of his country, thanks to a bloodless *coup d'etat* in 1772.

Gustav has gone down in Swedish history as the great patron of the arts and the theatre — he founded the Swedish Academy, for example — but personally he was overfond of intrigue, both on the stage and in everyday life, to such a degree that he must ultimately have muddled fact and fantasy. At all events, on leaving for a masked ball at the Opera in March 1792, he might well have been revelling in his airy plans of marching on Paris at the head of an army placed at his disposal by all the crowned heads of Europe to crush the French Revolution, for he quite overlooked a wide-ranging Swedish conspiracy against him, the fruit of years of work by a number of highly-placed civil and military aristocratic figures.

The conspiracy was a real cloak-and-dagger affair. During the ball masked men in cloaks surrounded the king, one of them uttered the password: "Good evening, beautiful mask!" and another discharged a pistol at the king, who cried out: *"Je suis blessé!"* Shouts on all sides of "fire!" had the guests rushing for the doors, but the guards kept their heads: they refused to let anyone leave who did not reveal their name.

The wounded king was carried out to his carriage, in which he was driven to the palace on the other side of Strömmen. A pair of pistols and a knife with a barbed blade were soon

The facade of Riddarhuset, the Palace of the Nobility, which took some twenty-five years to build from the start in 1641.

35

found; one of the pistols had apparently been fired at the king. The would-be assassin – a Captain Anckarström – was arrested by morning; he might now perhaps be commemorated by a statue somewhere in Stockholm, inscribed to the memory of a superlative patriot, had his shot killed the king outright.

But the king lived a further two weeks. The coup collapsed, its moving spirits were seized and either sent into exile or incarcerated. Anckarström was flogged in front of the House of the Nobility before being executed in the usual way outside Skanstull, where some of the foundation stones of his scaffold may still be seen in a peaceful little park in the midst of some apartment buildings.

Circumstances, predictably unpredictable, found the son of one of the exiles as head of the *Opéra Comique* in Paris, still in the lifetime of his father, some twenty years after the attempted regicide. This must have come to the ears of the suitably-named writer, Scribe, who wrote the libretto for Auber's successful opera *Gustave III ou Le Bal masqué*. Many years later, it formed the basis for the libretto for Verdi's *Un ballo in maschera* which, in 1859, was due to open in Naples. With Garibaldi just off stage, so to say, the censor would not permit the public representation of the murder of even a Swedish king, and ludicrous changes – Boston for Stockholm and an Earl of Warwick for Gustav III – were forced on the irritated composer.

Since the 1930s, however, this euphemistic treatment has been discontinued.

The building in which the masked ball was held was torn down at the turn of the 20th century, and the present opera house was built on the site. Across the square, the building that now houses the foreign ministry closely resembles the first opera house, for it was built in the 1780s with a façade to match that of the opera.

Gustav III was survived by a fourteen-year-old son. After a short regency, he ascended the throne in 1796 as Gustav IV Adolf. At this stage of the Napoleonic Wars, every state with a finger in the Baltic pie did its best to get a larger share through a bewildering variety of short-lived hostilities, ambiguous neutralities, armed pacts and coalitions. Neither Sweden nor Gustav IV emerged as very successful. Finland, having been an essential part of Sweden since the thirteenth century, seized this opportunity to free itself from Swedish control by seeking to become a Russian Grand Dutchy. By March 1809 Gustav IV was clearly losing control of his realm.

The actor Stellan Skarsgård as Gustav III, in a production at the Dramatic Theatre.

The opera house that existed in 1792 closely resembled this building, Arvfurstens palats, which now houses the Ministry of Foreign Affairs.

Seven decisive officers rushed the palace at dawn on the thirteenth. They locked the king in one of his rooms but overlooked a concealed door through which he escaped. They caught up with him before he could alarm the guards. He was declared deposed, and after a period of confinement in Sweden was sent into exile, as 'Colonel Gustafsson.' He died nearly thirty years later, in Switzerland.

No better successor could be found to this unhappy sovereign than one of his uncles, a decrepid childless roué of sixty one, who thus became Karl XIII of Sweden. He had never been the naval hero that a postumous statue in Kungsträdgården might suggest, and he had scarcely been crowned before he was unwillingly induced to ensure the succession by adopting a Danish prince as his heir. The prince, however, predeceased him, dying suddenly in the course of military manoevres in southern Sweden the following year. His body was brought to Stockholm for burial, and the funeral procession included the Earl Marshall of Sweden, Axel von Fersen.

This fifty-five-year-old aristocrat had achieved much in life. In youth he had won the regard of Gustav III, in his early twenties he had entered French service and seen action in the American War of Independence, and on returning to France in 1783, he found this romantic absence had not diminished him or his fine looks in the eyes of Marie Antoinette. He became her lover. He was also his king's personal agent at the French court. When Gustav III was deluding himself with plans of international action against revolutionary France, von Fersen had the job of extricating the French royal family from their imprisonment. At first

Seagull's view of the city on the water.

all went well: disguised as a coachman, he sprang his prisoners right under the noses of their guards. The flight to Varennes could begin.

His former mistress, however, would not content herself with a simple, light and rapid carriage, but insisted instead on something heavy, luxurious and slow. Von Fersen, at any rate, reached Brussels safely, where he continued in Gustav III's service. He later found favour with Gustav IV.

This was not forgotten when the Danish prince died so suddenly, especially not by those who favoured the succession of one of Gustav IV's sons. The Earl Marshall was rumoured to have had the prince poisoned, and the crowds who had gathered for the spectacle of the funeral, or the free beer and spirits which the inns were serving to mark the occasion, began to

shower his gilded coach with stones as it passed Slussen, the sluices at the southern end of the Old Town. The showers grew heavier as the procession swung into Stora Nygatan, which leads straight to Riddarhuset. The mob stopped his coach, pulled him out and began to beat him up. He tried to escape towards Riddarhuset, where a formation of troops was drawn up, in the presumable belief that they would come to his aid. However, they merely looked on as he was done to death.

It has never been satisfactorily explained who – if anyone – incited the crowd to violence, and why the military did nothing to stop it. Many in the crowd were those of the better sort, suitably disguised. Memoirs of the time suggest the king had a hand in the game, but whether or not anyone was exploiting the situation, feelings must have been easily inflamed

after the traumatic loss of Finland in 1809. The political and dynastic crisis was resolved with glorious success the following year: the second choice of a successor to Karl XIII, who by now was semi-senile, was a most happy one — Karl Johan Bernadotte, the eponymous founder of the present royal house of Sweden.

Here from Mosebacke we can in imagination follow *Wasa* on her unhappy maiden voyage on an August day in 1628. Planned as the largest Swedish man o' war, she had been partly built when rumours of an even larger Danish vessel reached Stockholm. No-one dared oppose Gus-

tavus Adolphus' response — a direct order to complete the new vessel with three, rather than the planned two, gun decks. She was inevitably unstable, and the inevitable took little time to occur.

About mid afternoon of the 28th, she was warped out from below the palace; off Slussen she hoisted a few sails and fired a salute. A few hundred metres further east, off Kastellholmen, a puff of wind struck the ship. She heeled, put her lowest gun ports under water, and never righted herself. Off Beckholmen, a few hundred metres further east, she simply sank

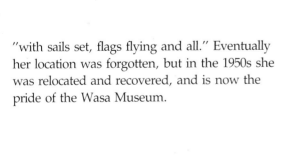

"with sails set, flags flying and all." Eventually her location was forgotten, but in the 1950s she was relocated and recovered, and is now the pride of the Wasa Museum.

From the South Side: Gröna Lund's look-out tower in the centre, and Kaknästornet, the highest structure in Scandinavia, in the background.

Fjällgatan, a street on the South Side.

The warship Wasa.

In the 1620s, when she was built, Sweden was a major power, and the Baltic virtually a Swedish lake. Masses of loot were carted home during the Thirty Years' War, and Drottningholm Palace, now the residence of the Swedish royal family, provides evidence of these successes. A walk in the palace gardens — partly open to the public — allows visitors to admire the great fountain and its sculptures, and other monuments, all of which were acquired, as the custom of the time approved, on the war-torn continent.

Today Sweden is a small country, and the eastern Baltic shores, once her possessions, have long since passed into other hands. Her capital, however, has become a large metropolis: when *Wasa* sank its population was only some 8,000. It rose to some 40,000 by 1700, to 75,000 by 1800, to 300,000 by 1900, and is now about a million. The city goes from strength to strength.

The royal family reside in
Drottningholm Palace.

Queen Silvia.

Create your own traditions

Ulla Winblad* still dances on the grass in front of the Bellman House, the long, red painted wooden building with its external gallery that may be seen immediately to the left of the main entrance to the oldest pleasure gardens in Sweden.

Here, perhaps, lay a part of the Gröna Lund Inn that was so popular in Bellman's days. While the inn dates in part from the mid-eighteenth century, the pleasure gardens themselves opened in 1883. Since 1938, 26 July is celebrated as the traditional Bellman Day.

The pleasure gardens' summer traditions include the presentation of the Jussi Björling* Stipendium, an appearance on the Main Scene by Sven-Bertil Taube*, following those of his celebrated father. The public has its own traditions, on the dance floor, in the House of Mirrors, at that outburst of meglomania, Tyrol, that has been considered ugly ever since it was built in the 1930s, on the Giant Ferris Wheel and the merry-go-rounds, at the ball and dart stands, in front of the Main Scene.

The management has the traditions of a family company, now in its fourth generation. Jakob Schultheis, the founder, was followed by his son Gustaf Nilsson, whose widow, Nadeshda Nilsson, ran it until her daughter Ninni married the Lundgren who ran the competing establishment (Lundgren's Pleasure Grounds) over the road and united the families' fortunes. They are now run by John Lindgren Jnr and his relatives and employees.

What started as a small confined pleasure gardens by the Bellman House on one side of

the road − Lilla Allmänna Gränd − now extends along the waters of Stockholms Ström, where today the fun of the fair has the Rollercoaster as its main attraction.

Evening approaches, and the lights begin to shine in the tower, in the restaurants, on the housey-housey stalls, on the train, the cars, along the quays and over the water. And "There's Gröna Lund," say people on Fjällgatan, watching the ferries cross the Stockholm waters with passengers for the pleasure gardens. Autumn and winter follow, carpentry and building for the new season begin, while people in the office draw up contracts with artists, compose programmes and design posters. As spring comes, 40,000 bulbs begin to shoot as the doors open for the season's premiere. Many would like to forget the year it snowed!

And Gröna Lund lives with its new and old traditions. And Ulla Winblad still dances on the grass while Bellman himself peers out over Bellmansro.

The brewer himself checks the strength of the wort.

The spring at Vårby

The spring at Vårby is known from archeological evidence to have been used by people on this beautiful arm of the Mälar Lake from the end of the Viking period. In the 17th century, it gave "the cleanest water of all the springs of the neighbourhood;" Urban Hjärne* hymned its water as "clear and transparent as the finest crystal; in the glass it reveals innumerable tiny bubbles like pearls or fresh wine. Its taste is delightful, with hidden acidity." In 1708, he got it classed as a medicinal spa, and royalty and other persons drank its water to cure many maladies, including hysteria and melancholy. It was soon sold by Stockholm apothecaries. The court received a supply every other day.

Later a mineral-water factory was built there. Today, Wårby Källa — one of the largest and most modern breweries in Sweden — is owned by the Cooperative Movement and produces more than 75m litres of a complete range of beers, mineral waters and other soft drinks annually. Every day, 1m 33cl bottles are shipped from Wårby Källa to every part of Sweden — primarily to cooperative shops and stores, but also increasingly to state-run liquor stores, restaurants and staff canteens, hospitals and other public-service institutions, and kiosks and fast-food stalls.

Nowadays, when most things are artificial, good water can be got only from wholly natural sources. The spring at Vårby is a unique and unexcelled asset, gushing with 144,000 litres of water a day. This meets about one third of the brewery's needs, being used foremost for different mineral waters and to produce *Pepsi-Cola* under licence.

There are many signs that mineral water is increasing in popularity. Swedes have rediscovered it and now drink 7 litres a year each. This is more than we once did, but still far short of the French figure, which is ten times the size!

Like an artesian well, water once gushed from the earth at Vårby, the spring that has given 6,000 litres clear bubbling water an hour for centuries. Today, the spring is well hidden and secured under lock and key, behind the small temple in the foreground.

A DYNAMIC CENTRE:
Stockholm as a financial market place

Like the other northern capitals, Stockholm is a real capital, that's to say the seat of power of the country's political and economic establishments.

Only a few minutes' walk from the Palace lie the government offices, the *riksdag*, the palatial head offices of the principal banks, the Stock Exchange and the crown jewels of culture − the Royal Opera, the Royal Dramatic Theatre and the National Museum. The spirits of finance and culture amicably share the Stock Exchange building, which houses the Stock Exchange itself and the Nobel-prize awarding Swedish Academy. So intricately woven is the tapestry of Swedish life. Different powers meet in the Swedish synthesis − a shared political understanding of the mixed economy that provides the foundation for Swedish well-being.

Representatives of financial dynasties such as the Wallenbergs and the Johnsons dine at the Palace beside company directors, politicians of different political colours, scientists and cultural personages.

The larger Swedish industries located around, even in, the kernel of the capital include Ericsson, Elektrolux, AlfaLaval, Atlas Copco, Fläkt, Aga. Relatively smaller companies are found here too, either serving the large companies or occupying some niche that provides them with an international market. Together with service and trading companies, they form the Stockholm financial marketplace.

For many long years, the powers of Swedish business met in a partly enclosed world encompassed by a few bank headquarters and board rooms, while their companies' goods and products enjoyed an international reputation. The economically and financially flourishing 1980s afforded space for new powers to grow, and Mother Svea − that buxom personification of Sweden − opened her arms to the world around her, and the world came to lodge in Mother Svea's capacious bosom or, more prosaically, in Stockholm.

This new spirit, this optimism about the future, found expression in part in the stock-market boom. By the later 1980s, Stockholm Stock Exchange prices were more than eight times their level in 1980, a record no other stock-market could match, and bankers and investors travelled to Stockholm to see, and hear, and buy shares.

Stockholm's own financial centre grew up in the blocks around Kungsträdgården which, earlier, had been dominated by the three big banks − Skandinaviska Enskilda Banken, Svenska Handelsbanken and PK Banken. Foreign banks were admitted. The number of stockmarket firms doubled in the course of a few years to about thirty. New and old dealers developed into merchant banks. Options and futures were traded in entirely new premises. The total volume of business reached billions of Swedish crowns.

When the recoil struck, stock-markets all over the world were affected, Stockholm along with Wall Street and the City of London. Restructuring operations already begun in Stockholm were accelerated, but the new financial centre had been equipped to operate both with rising and falling prices.

"What we have seen so far is only the beginning of the development of a City of Stockholm," states Bengt Rydén, Director of the Stockholm Stock Exchange, which has its own Big Bang in preparation − a wholly computerised dealing system.

He points out that many foreign interests can be expected to enter the Swedish securities market, that the Stockholm Stock Exchange is experiencing only the early stages of a larger wave of privatising, in which state-owned, cooperative and local-government companies issue shares on the market.

There's much yet to do in financial Stockholm. A financial market's most vital job is to channel capital to companies and people able to put it to work in new production, trade and services, thus contributing to the development of an even better society. On the following pages we give some examples of just such people and companies.

"How's ASEA today?" Young dealers in ancient surroundings: the premises house not only the Stock Market but also the Swedish Academy.

"The dollar's gone up to-day!" while a customer waits on the phone for a deal to be concluded quickly. This is in Nordbank's trading room in the new NK office premises.

Stockholm as a place of business
Where people meet and business is done

Nothing can reduce the importance in social or business life of meetings between people, nor the importance of the right surroundings and atmosphere for them. Stockholm is fortunate in its natural landscape, its islands and holms, the rocky outcrops along the edge of fresh and salt waters, and the flat lands between them. This is the landscape of the Mälar lake, which has provided the communications of the trading centres of Sweden Proper as they have grown and developed: Helgö until the late eighth century, Birka – now Björkö – until nearly the year 1000, and then Sigtuna and Uppsala, before Stockholm became the largest and indisputably most important town of the area.

Goods, often from faraway countries, were traded at these markets, which also provided local services. Many markets still exist in Stockholm, some traditionally in market squares, others in department stores and shops, others again as exhibitions, fairs, conferences and congresses, where ideas as much as goods and services are exchanged. Some 200 venues for conferences and congresses exist in the Greater Stockholm area, and participants can choose among 150 hotels, which together have 23,000 beds.

As to goods, Stockholm is richly endowed with market places. In the inner city there are big department stores and specialist shops and boutiques, and further out from the centre are shopping centres, supermarkets and trade fairs. Despite the massive expansion of business in the suburbs, downtown Stockholm has held its position as Sweden's commercial centre. It's here the new trends, the new fashions and the new goods are first snapped up, to be spread later over the whole country. This is especially so in the clothing business, which has a central concentration of mode-creating shops and stores.

On account of their size, trade fairs have located some way from the centre. The largest is the Stockholm Trade Fairs' premises at Älvsjö, with 9,000 seats for conferences and the like; its million visitors a year enjoy the planned and spontaneous meetings that take place on its premises.

In a word, no modern technique or device can provide a substitute for what we feel when we meet.

The Stockholm Trade Fairs are visited by 1m people annually.

A big fair and Stockholm's largest congress centre

A place of contact where sellers and buyers meet over what's new — that's the function of the Stockholm International Fairs.

Trade fairs are an increasingly tough international business, and investments in fairs increase faster than their total volume of business. They grow in number, often through division into specialised fairs, although new industries — for example, electronics and computers — generate wholly new fairs.

Instead of competing with the biggest fairs in the world, Stockholm has backed a couple of leading international events, and some forty recurrent fairs of mainly Swedish interest. In total, Stockholm is the choice of some fifty annual or bi-annual fairs, with an immense range of interests — boats, motorcycles, dogs, antiques,

domestic foodstuffs, plus nonconsumer fairs for computers, technology, medicine, fashion and furniture. Then there's the Motor Show, and fairs for earth-shifting machinery, local-government work, and hotels and restaurants.

Exhibition areas in five halls now total nearly 40,000 square metres, with services occupying as much again. The adjoining congress centre is the largest in Sweden; its 26 rooms can seat 8,000 people, the largest seating 3,350! Over 1,300 congresses, seminars, conferences, and other meetings are arranged annually. Some ten eating places — from a first-class restaurant to cafeterias — can serve up to 2,000 people at a time.

The Fairs have unintentionally become a large-scale entertainment centre, for example,

Large and small objects are on exhibition at the fifty or so trade fairs that fill the annual calendar of the Swedish Trade Fairs. From the Building Contractors' Fair.

for companies' inauguration events, anniver-
sary banquets and the like.

Altogether visitors number about 1.3m so,
not surprisingly, big Stockholm hotels check
the International Fairs' programme when planning their own activities.

*Some 35 trade and public fairs are held each year, and
nearly 10,000 companies from all over the world are
represented.*

*There are many ways to show products, and the
Stockholm premises are flexible, and can always meet
customers' needs.*

*About 160,000 people come annually to the Stock-
holm Conference Centre, to see, hear and learn, and
sometimes to enjoy themselves at companies' parties.*

Helping exporters trade goods for goods

As everyone knows, trade can be carried on in various ways. In SUKAB's offices, with their views over Humlegården, the Royal Library and the statue of Carl von Linneus*, a very special form of trade is carried on, namely countertrade. In Swedish, the company's name means 'The Swedish Countertrade Company Limited,' and its centrally-located offices are a meeting place for businessmen and traders from all over the world.

Countertrade can be carried on in many ways, and the following example nicely illustrates how the method can satisfy highly divergent interests: SUKAB successfully arranged · that exports of mining equipment from Sweden to North Korea, a country with a shortage of foreign currency, were traded for cement, which was traded for pig iron from Pakistan, which was traded for jute from Bangladesh that was then traded for nuts from Mozambique that were delivered to their purchaser in the UK, whose payment could be accepted by the original exporter in Sweden.

SUKAB has countertrade agreements with many countries and also combines project-financing solutions with countertrade. An example was a delivery by Volvo of vehicles costing $8m to Pakistan. Thanks to a countertrade agreement, the buyer paid SUKAB in Pakistani currency over five years and Volvo was paid on delivery in Swedish currency by SUKAB. The credit to Pakistan was re-financed through a bank and repaid from funds generated by exports from Pakistan during these five years.

SUKAB's product is thus convertible currency from barter and countertrade transactions that may be complex but which can open vital import sources and/or export markets to debt-burdened third-world countries. In the opposite direction, so to say, exporting industrial companies can sell on markets otherwise closed to them by hard-currency shortages. SUKAB is unique in being owned by some eighty Swedish export companies and, through the Swedish Investment Bank, partly by the Swedish state. This semi-official status, however, does not restrict it to business affecting only Sweden. Many developing countries use its expertise in their marketing, while industries in Sweden use it for what is called offset business: combining, for example, an export of high-tech equipment on condition that the seller undertakes to provide technical assistance, sub-contracting and the like.

SUKAB's offices in Stockholm function as the information and communication centre for countertrade business all over the world.

The principles of countertrade business are often worked out at diplomatic level. The Commercial Councillor and the Commercial Attaché of the Stockholm Embassy of the Peoples' Republic of China are seen here in discussion with SUKAB's managing director.

IKEA's store at Kungens Kurva is a mecca for furniture shoppers and, with 3m visitors annually, the most popular single excursion attraction for Stockholmers.

The open-air market at Farsta Centrum, one of Stockholm's modern suburban centres.

Boutiques, stores, sales... all on Drottninggatan, the classic shopping street in central Stockholm.

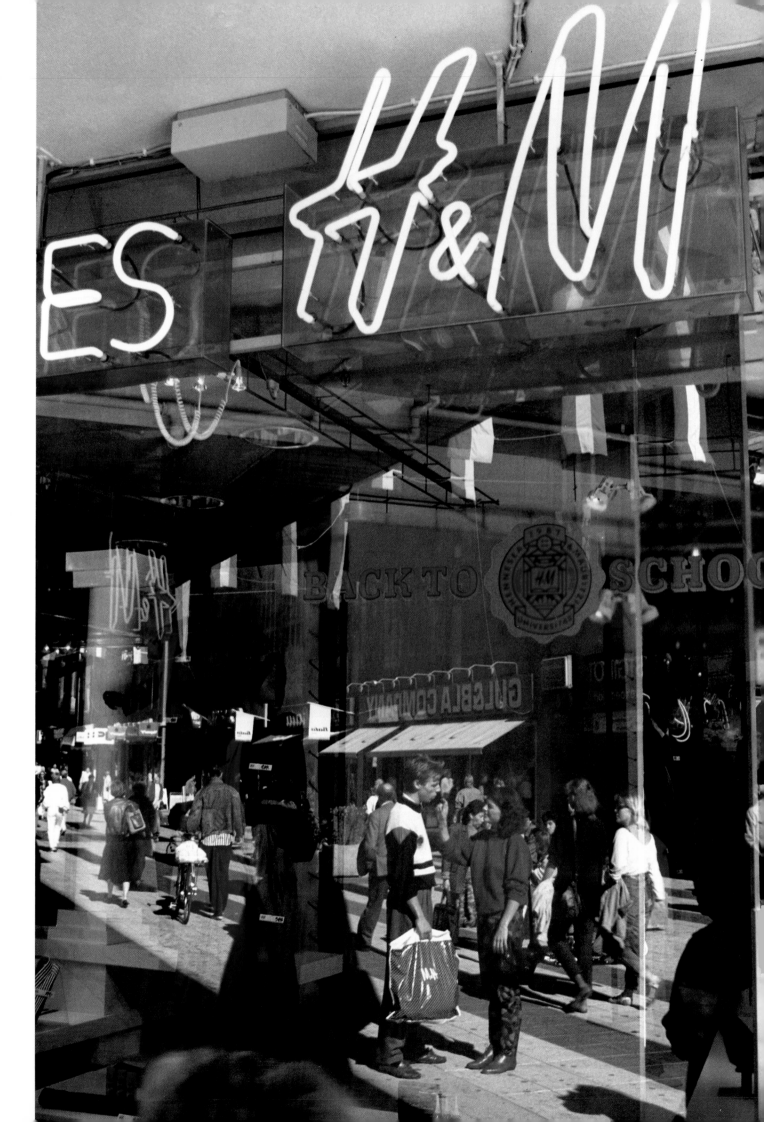

An old-fashioned shopping street — now a pedestrian precinct — in Sigtuna, one of the oldest towns in Sweden; it's quite close to Arlanda.

The mirror of a pulsing big city: youth, neon lights, the latest mode...

and the great store, built in granite.

The heady perfume of the fine world

Not only the Perfume Department of NK is pervaded by the scent of the fine world. Ever since the massive building in Bohuslän granite on Hamngatan opened in 1915, the whole store has been the cult place for people in Stockholm — Swedes from all over Sweden, and others from all over the world — who want 'first-class shopping' for birthdays and Christmas presents: clothes, furnishings, cosmetics, jewellery, furs, sport and leisure equipment, glass, porcelain, kitchen equipment, books, and naturally foodstuffs.

Everything is to be found here, not only some 200,000 different articles, but a wide range of services: from hairdressing and beauty salons, to a travel agency, an export service and excellent eating places.

And history has gone full circle. AB Nordiska Kompaniet was founded in 1902 when the two largest retailers in Stockholm, K.M. Lundberg and Joseph Leja, amalgamated their businesses. On moving to Hamngatan, Lundberg sold his premises at Stureplan, to Axel

Ax:son Johnson*; they have since been the head office for the Johnson Group* and Nordstjernan*. NK and the Johnson Group met again in 1983, the year Nordstjernan became the majority shareholder in NK.

It's now a conglomerate of department stores in Göteborg and Malmö, and of course Stockholm, of fashion clothes in Täby and Farsta, and companies for interior design and property; its turnover is measured in milliards of crowns. As it turned out, the huge store on Hamngatan contained something almost more sought after than the goods for sale — vacant premises, great dusty store rooms, old, hardworn staff canteens high up in the building where customers never penetrated.

So mode-conscious NK entered the property boom, through the door to Regeringsgatan Number 18, a street crossing Hamngatan. Ragnar Uppman* created new light wells and small squares, revealed the staircase by Asplund*, called for marble floors and polished brass in a display of architectural haute couture.

And bankers, financiers and dealers in options and securities moved in. Seldom has NK and its personnel and goods caught the tide at its flood so precisely as during the latter part of the 1980s.

But nostalgic feelings suit habituées of the NK restaurant which, being subject to a preservation order, still looks as it did when Ferdinand Boberg* created it, when its panelling was newly chiselled. One can order one's 'biff Greta,' named for a managing director's secretary, and discreetly take an NK *bisquit* with coffee. 'That's very good taste, indeed . . . '

The Boberg Room of the NK Restaurant is the meeting place of businessmen and shoppers. Food culture and architectural culture meet here, too.

You can visit openings of art exhibitions at NK.

Are they everywhere?

Anyone strolling through Stockholm can easily feel Hennes & Mauritz is everywhere. There's something in that, for H&M expands constantly and has acquired twenty five of the best shopping premises in the town. It's hard not to notice them − things are always happening in and around them, in their display windows, and their whole style.

Even since 1947, when the company started business, it's gone for low prices, but since then this has been sharpened. The group contains units which compete even with exclusive special boutiques, offering the lowest prices in each segment of the market: "Impuls" for teenagers, "Uptown" for demanding male customers, "Puls" for sporting types, and "BK" for fashion-conscious ladies.

H&M is now one of the leading European fashion retailers, and of course the largest in Scandinavia. This naturally gives important advantages of scale, not least in purchasing, where volume and prices are strongly connected. It's also a strong argument, when H&M pressures suppliers to show low prices don't have to mean lowered quality.

Market dominance can easily lead to over-boldness, but H&M has been careful to guard against a role as trend setter. The head office in Stockholm never tries to decree tomorrow's mode − on the contrary, market signals are watched and listened to carefully. The whole organisation is kept as flexible as possible, so H&M can always be first with what's new. Buyers learn a few mistakes are allowed − anyone frightened of putting a foot wrong soon stands still all day long, but in the fashion business one must be daring.

An important source of information in Sweden are the group's many shops in continental Europe, where much that's new appears before it reaches Sweden. Fashion flows the other way, too, and H&M has become one of Sweden's largest exporters of textile products − to its own shops! Expansion continues, but only as internal financing and undiminished profitability allow. With turnover approaching SEK 5,000m there's little to gain from simply increasing sales volume. But the group intends both to expand, and to keep on developing its nearly 200 shops.

H&M has many profiles for its customers: the BK Shop on Hamngatan specialises in up-market styles.

Keeping in the swim of current fashion, maintaining quality and form...

...never following mere routine in purchasing. Creative discussions of the planning and coordination of buying are vital to H&M.

Working in Stockholm
A melting pot of jobs

The Greater Stockholm region, with nearly 1.5m people, contains nearly 17% of the population of Sweden, and provides nearly 900,000 jobs, or over 20% of the national total. Its job market, however, is naturally metropolitan, for the region is home to countless national centres of administration of public and private entities.

For example, over 50% of Sweden's managing directors live in the region, as do most economists (70%), engineers (60%), architects (75%) and bank directors (45%). The public sector accounts for almost 40% of all Stockholm jobs and 37% of those of the whole country. For retail trade, the figures are 18% (14% nationally); for banking, insurance and the like 15% (8%); for the building industry almost 4% (6%); but for manufacturing industry, the figures are 13% in Stockholm, but 24% nationally. The other marked difference is in banking, insurance and similar services.

Even so, several of the big Swedish export industries have head offices and factories in the region: they include Electrolux, Ericsson, Atlas Copco, Alfa-Laval, Fläkt and Aga. They have in turn created a living, and a lively industrial and technical environment, for many other, relatively smaller industrial, trading and service companies.

According to Harry Faulkner, Managing Director of the international Alfa-Laval Group: "The trend is for industry to move to the suburbs or elsewhere in Sweden. Stockholm is becoming more and more a centre for company management, and financial and service activities." Alfa-Laval's previous head office lay in Tumba, just south of Stockholm; the Group still has considerable facilities there and, of its 16,000 employees in Sweden, 2,500 work in the Stockholm region. The Group has an annual turnover of some SEK 12,000m; its management has recently moved into central Stockholm. "We want to be in closer contact with the financial world in Stockholm," says Harry Faulkner.

Alfa-Laval has recently made a further move in its general internationalisation by opening a financial office in Brussels. It's part of a pattern to be observed in several large Swedish companies.

Can Stockholm be getting too small as a base for companies of Alfa-Laval's sort? Faulkner

shakes his head. "Our activities are managed from our head office in Stockholm. And if Sweden accomodates to the internationalisation of financial markets and trade politics, Stockholm could continue to be a dynamic base for head offices and financial management, and a home for new and expansive companies in, for example, high technology and services."

Going home from one of Stockholm's largest employers, L.M. Ericsson.

Made in Swedem – by IBM!

Planning, research, education, economics, information, health care, administration, technology, manufacturing – just about every function of modern society depends on computers. And wherever there are computers, there's IBM.

Of IBM's thirteen factories in Europe, one lies in Järfälla. It once made typewriters and punched-card machines, but its accumulated skills are now employed in making computer-system printers, which contain much mechanical action, and disk-drive control units. The factory is naturally highly computerised, using CAD/CAM, robots, driverless trucks etc.

IBM Svenska AB, exporting annually some SEK 3,500m, is one of Sweden's top-twenty exporters, with customers in over 120 countries. Its production is so rationalised that, despite high costs, it still does well against the well-known tough internal IBM competition; indeed, Järfälla is the only source of some IBM products.

IBM Nordiska Laboratorier, on Lidingö, is one of IBM's four European centers for program development – the fastest growing part of the business. Its specialities are systems and programs for accounting, budgetting and other financial functions, and man/machine communications, especially for users who know little about computers. Its ambition is to produce simple but yet powerful tools for computing and information retrieval. In total, exports from Järfälla and Lidingö account for about half the turnover of IBM Svenska AB.

Computer technology continues its rapid development. Customers and users, on the one hand, and IBM people, on the other need comprehensive education and training. IBM's Training Center has over 80,000 student days per annum – half for IBM people and half for their customers – which makes IBM one of the country's largest private educators.

Once a small workshop, this highly computerised IBM factory makes printers and disk-drive control units.

(Far right) IBM's Training Center provides over 80,000 student days annually.

(Right) IBM computers at the hospital-services administration of the county of Stockholm.

Handwork and high technology

When the former director-general of Televerket retired he received from his company what was probably the world's first telephone made of hardwood. This idea gave birth to one of Teli AB's new niche products.

Teli, once the industrial division of Televerket, is now an independently operating subsidiary in the Swedish Televerk Group. It now actively markets products and services outside the Group, which had been its main customer previously, with the aim of bringing external sales up to about half total turnover.

All this has demanded complete mental adjustment and the build up of a sales network abroad aimed primarily at markets in the other Nordic countries, in the UK and the USA. There's a subsidiary in Singapore. Teli has supplied an automatic-data-processing system to the New Zealand telephone administration.

Teli is an advanced telecommunications and electronics company with a wide range of services and products: telephones, terminals and exchanges, networks (AXE is the Swedish name of its principal component), traffic-control systems, automatic-data-processing and training systems, and individual components such as PC boards.

The exclusive telephones are sold in Harrods and other shops in the UK, while both the UK and the USA are important markets for Teli's general telephones and terminals.

Teli is otherwise well established on the world market as a supplier of traffic-control systems, having a large part of the total flight market. The Garex and Stratus systems provide integrated coordinated central control of communications via radio, telephones and intercoms, not just for flight control but also for marine, police, fire-fighting and rescue services. For alarm centres there is the wholly integrated Coordcom system.

With a human-capital concentration of knowledge, Teli has specialised in computer-supported training systems; its subsidiary Tele-Nova is the centre for these operations. DataNova, Teli's joint-venture company with the Swedish Esselte Group, is responsible for developing the market in Sweden for computed-supported training.

With its computers, Teli now dominates the supply of computerised training systems to Swedish schools. The company is now raising its ambitions to enter the market for computer-supported assistance for the handicapped.

A successful maker of systems to raise individuals' levels of knowledge has naturally a high-technological and effective production of its own. An extra card up Teli's sleeve is its new factory for PC boards for supply to external and internal customers. As always, the small details are often of crucial importance.

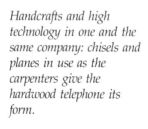

Handcrafts and high technology in one and the same company: chisels and planes in use as the carpenters give the hardwood telephone its form.

By contrast, the very latest and most complex modern techniques are needed to produce miniaturised electronics components for telecommunications.

The porcelain factory as a tourist attraction

One of Stockholm's most popular excursion goals is in fact an old manufacturing company. Every year more than 100,000 persons make the journey out to tradition-rich Gustavsberg on Värmdö, an island in the Stockholm skerries. They come to look at fine old porcelain, to admire the skills of the potters, and of course to make purchases in the shop.

The visitors wander round in the Ceramics Center and learn that the whole began as early as 1825, when the Board of Commerce gave its permission for a "Factory for miscellaneous Porcelain Goods." They may see how designers of different times left their mark on the products — right up to ideas for designs that are yet only at the testing stage.

"But, yes, of course," is perhaps the most frequent comment in the exhibition that recalls that today's Gustavsberg is foremost active in the sanitary-porcelain industry. Gustavsberg's sanitary porcelain is to be found in a large number of Swedish homes.

Expressions become more perplexed in front of the exhibition stands that show parts of pipes and pumps. What has all this to do with the elegant table services? Well, there really is a link. During the time the industry has been owned by KF Industri AB (part of the Swedish Cooperative Movement), it has broadened its activities step by step.

With porcelain as a basis, production of sanitary porcelain began in 1939. It was soon natural to complement this with enamelled steel-sheet baths. Water thus became a common denominator for Gustavsberg's activities which now include the production of everything from pipes and pumps to baths, showers, toilets, kitchen sinks, mixers and so on.

In the little community of Gustavsberg we can today meet three separate companies — Gustavsberg VVS AB (sanitary porcelain and so on), Gustavsberg Fastigheter AB (a property company), and the newly-amalgamated Rörstrand-Gustavsberg AB (domestic porcelain).

Gustavsberg as a company has its origins in a brickworks founded during the 1640s by Gustav Gabrielsson Oxenstierna* and his wife Marie De la Gardie*. Since then the company has been a large owner of land and buildings in the community. In this capacity Gustavsberg Fastigheter AB has begun to devote resources to a large tourist project, where the unique skerries environment is to be cared for and made accessible to the general public. Much suggests many more visitors will come to Gustavsberg in the future.

A skerries' steamer provides a popular way to reach Gustavsberg from central Stockholm.

Gustavsberg was first known as a maker of fine porcelain china. Nowadays sanitary procelain goods are mass produced.

The skills of throwing, painting and finishing Gustavsberg's classic Blå Blom service are demonstrated. Visitors can also try painting porcelain.

Some of the more remarkable creations of Gustavsberg's 160 years of porcelain making are on display in the Ceramics Center.

A company with several dimensions

To shape or form a piece of metal the point to be machined must be determined precisely in terms of length, width and height; a technically-minded person would speak of its x, y, and z coordinates, its three dimensions, its three 'Reference sides.' Börje Ramsbro had this in mind when he named his company 'System 3R.'

Metal can be worked in many ways. System 3R has specialised in equipment and solutions for spark erosion, a technique used for highly precise treatment of, for example, metallic substances to make moulds for the plastics industry. The spark bores, cuts, 'planes,' and even 'polishes' surfaces to mirror smoothness, if need be to the nearest thousandth of a millimetre or even finer. Take a look at a telephone handset or the Fiskars scissors, the ones with the orange plastic handles: they have most probably been formed from plastic injected into a mould spark-eroded with equipment and technology from System 3R.

System 3R's product range includes some 500

items: components for manufacturing and positioning electrodes, equipment for positioning the item to be worked, electronic control equipment and computer programs are only some of them.

In other words, System 3R is a highly specialised niche company; it originated in 1968, when Börje Ramsbro sat at home in Spånga, making drawings of electrodes and various ways of positioning and guiding them. Today, the company's head office in Vällingby is the base for an industrial group of sixteen companies, spread all over the world, with some 300 employees. Of its 1987 turnover of about SEK 200m, over 90% was exported.

Börje Ramsbro is an entrepreneur and technician who takes part in public discussion of issues of the day. In formulating his management philosophy, he naturally sums it up as 'the Three R's:' Risk-taking, Realism, Results. The company is organised not hierachically but in accordance with a three-sided chart.

A scrupulously careful final inspection is only to be
expected for products made to the nearest thousandth
of a millimetre.

People and technology meet here. All final assembly
of System 3R's products is done at the principal factory in Vällingby.

Orbiting, or planetary spark erosion, with a radial
movement of a few tenths of a millimetre.

   It is, then, a systematically applied philosophy of management that goes hand in hand
with the technical realities of everyday work, in
a perspective that extends beyond the horizons
of System 3R and Vällingby. In a motto, "The
Five Dimensions of Reality," are encapsuled the
words "3R in keeping with the individual."

The art or craft of printing money

Great precision is needed to produce any printing plate, but one for postage stamps, for example, must comprise several hundred identical impressions. It demands minute attention and the very greatest and most uniform precision. An error of only one or two hundredths of a millimetre causes images to become unclear and colours to be wrong.

Generations of engravers and printers had created their own highly inventive handcopying methods, when two young Estonian engineers, Albert Meerik and Hatvig Soe, started a company in the early 1950s to make automatic copying machines. One of their first customers was Esselte, the large, influential Swedish Lithographical Company, which gave their machine thorough tests — and high marks. Misomex won an excellent name. Only a couple of years later, exports began from its small premises in Fruängen.

The machines were used first by printers of labels, coupons, bank notes and so on, a particular niche that widened with the growing use of four-colour printing: the same image must be printed exactly the same four times, each with a different colour. Misomex' automatic plate-making machines are used today by many modern printshops, including virtually all printers of bank notes, and naturally those of the Bank of Sweden, at Tumba.

In time, Misomex machines were discovered by other branches of industry, among them the printed-circuit industry, in which high-precision copying is needed. A further step was to make films for microscopic integrated circuits; Texas Instruments is still among Misomex' customers.

Today Misomex is one of the two or three leaders of this typical niche industry, and its products cover a large part of the market. Of an annual production of some 250 machines, some 97% are exported.

A niche product on its way to its world market. At least one machine leaves the assembly hall at Fruängen daily.

Immediately before printing this news-paper, the plates are given a final inspection.

These are the presses shared by Dagens Nyheter *and* Expressen, *a daily and an afternoon paper respectively.*

The oldest printing method became an art

Traditional screen printing, in which relatively thick opaque ink is pressed through fabric, gives results that artists have always favoured, but the method was scarcely used commercially other than by sign painters who rarely used anything except primitive equipment.

Printing technology developed, but screen printing remained a handcraft until the 1950s, when a Swedish pioneer, Åke Svantesson, began to make machines to mass produce screen work. Today his company, Svecia, makes machines that print up to 4,000 impressions per hour.

The re-discovered method has developed very rapidly, and the numbers of models of machines have increased from five to over sixty in only a few years; new models appear constantly. The designers at Svecia are now rarely surprised at anything, for they have been asked to produce machines to print almost everything: circuits for the electronics industry, heating conductors for car rear windows, declarations of content on sausage skins, decorations on cakes, butter on sandwiches, scented ink on perfume packages, trademarks and size numbers on the soles of shoes, ensyzmes on medical testing needles, patterns on interior panels in airplanes, emblems on police cars, flowers on Sevres porcelain.

One thing leads to another, and new ideas are born all the time. Could metal foil gaskets be printed and etched, rather than punched out? Could glue be printed with great accuracy, instead of being brushed on by hand, not very accurately? Of course!

But images on paper are still the dominating product, and as demands for accurate reproduction of colour grow, the screen-printing

The exterior and the interior of the Svecia head office and factory at Botkyrka, south of Stockholm.

A silkscreen press at a printers in France.

method increases in use. The printing industry in Sweden is well to the fore, and has obliged its suppliers of machinery to keep up. Svecia is today the world's leading maker of machines for screen printing and exports over 90% of its production. Its factory lies in Botkyrka, south of Stockholm, and has an area of 25,000 square metres.

Sweden's daily yeast

Without yeast there's no bread, and as bread is something no-one can do without, Sweden, like all other countries, needs its own production facilties.

The country's only factory is located at Rotebro, north of Stockholm, where a yeast factory was erected in the early 1890s. The present factory is new, having started production in 1980. It produces both fresh and dried yeast, and one third of its annual production of 18,000 tons goes to domestic customers, and the rest to bakers.

The factory is owned and managed by Jäst-bolaget AB, a company representing private and cooperative baking interests and the Swedish state.

Although yeast is really a very simple everyday product, its production calls for highly skilled biochemical techniques. This is one reason why Jästbolaget participates in research work together with colleges of further education and universities, in addition to pursuing its own research. One goal is to improve methods of production, another is to develop new sorts of yeast, a third is to find new products for new markets.

For over a century, yeast has been produced here — on the western shore of Norrviken, north of Stockholm — in a succession of factories, of which this is the latest.

The Marabou factory in Sundbyberg is distinguished by its exceptionally fine collection of European sculpture. This work is by the Italian sculptor, Marino Marini.

A DYNAMIC CENTRE:
Services in Stockholm

A large city like Stockholm functions well thanks to a well-developed network of services: communications, schools, hospitals, care of children and the elderly, energy supplies, water and sewage, refuse collection, police and fire-fighting services and so on. The Stockholm region contains many highly-developed services available from public and private bodies.

Arlanda, Europe's third busiest airport, is one example, and the public-service surface transport system is another. Stockholmers have the urban rail system – partly underground, partly on the surface, and called the *tunnelbana* – that is the largest in the world in proportion to the population it serves. It has a total length of 110 kilometres. Together with commuter-train services, buses and a short tramway, it sells some 2m journeys on an average working day.

An invisible communications network, too, is served through Televerket Radio's Kaknästornet, that essential feature of the Stockholm skyline. This includes radio and TV programmes, and telecommunications for telephones and computers, including the world's geographically most extensive mobile telephone system.

Stockholms Energiverk is Sweden's largest power-distribution company. Stockholm Water Works uses the most modern techniques to supply the town with fine drinking water and, through its sewage-disposal techniques and system, to make bathing and fishing possible right in the centre of the city. In addition, services are available from very many private companies in the transport, refuse-disposal, industrial and computer and electronics sectors.

This partly underground railway system, 110 km long, links Stockholm and its suburbs. In relation to their population, it is the most extensive urban railway network in the world.

When a new station is proposed, an artist is asked to add his or her contribution to 'the world's longest art exhibition.' So far more than 70 artists' work has enlivened stations on the tunnelbana.

Third busiest airport in Europe

An enchanted realm in the woods, a symbol of
Swedish isolation in northern forests, seen first
through cloud breaks – is this Ultima Thule, or
The Gateway to Sweden? Arlanda's runways
and terminal buildings, set in dark green summer forests or endless expanses of winter
white, form one of the larger European airports, the destination of many international
flights, the main link between international and
Swedish domestic services.

With fewer landings in Europe than only
Heathrow and Frankfurt, Arlanda sees 210,000
landings and take-offs, and 12m passengers
pass through its terminals, each year. Like
Sweden herself, Arlanda must cope with isolation and severe winters, but in doing so has become an international example of rationalised

technology, service and administration on a
human scale – most facilities are within walking
distance of each other.

Some 150 places of work here employ 10,000
people: hotels, restaurants, conference centres,
boutiques, shops, workshops, hangers, freight
and post terminals, a fire service – a whole
miniature society which never stops growing,
perhaps because it never sleeps.

The first scheduled arrival is Thai TG 920
from Bankok at 0600, and the last departure is
Swiss Air 412 to Helsinki at 2300. In between,
flights come and go to and from all parts of the
world: New York, Moscow, Frankfurt, Berlin,
Warsaw, Milan, London, Paris, Leningrad,
Bangkok . . . . Arlanda links east and west:
Aeroflot, Pan Am, Thai, and others, in total

some fifty airlines, use Arlanda, with SAS as naturally dominant.

Charter and freight flights begin when the scheduled flights have ended. In workshops mechanics service planes and motors, while freight forwarders and postal sorters work round the clock. In snow storms, airport employees, or local farmers on call, drive snow ploughs to keep runways and taxiing aprons usable – it takes a lot of snow to close Arlanda, even temporarily.

On the airport itself, domestic and international terminals are already planned and a third runway is to be laid; around the airport, where many new buildings are always appearing, more hotels and offices and the like will be built. The effect spreads out, towards Stock-

holm to the south, towards Uppsala to the north, like lines of force in a magnetic field, somewhere in the woods, only half an hour from central Stockholm.

Express postal links with all the world

A daily EMS flight leaves Arlanda at 2100 for the Brussels sorting office for express freight within Europe, and between Europe and New York. By midnight it's a scene of febrile activity, as express-freight planes fly in and land, as cargoes are off-loaded, sorted, reloaded for return flights to ten or more destinations. By noon, or less than twelve hours later, most items have reached their addressees — delivered to the door. These night flights are an important part of the gigantic work of transportation that's called EMS.

The EMS transportation network moves goods and documents internationally in a door-to-door service. It guarantees overnight delivery between New York and much of Europe, and within most of Europe; and delivery within

three days between most of Europe and Japan, China, Taiwan, South Korea, Hong Kong and other destinations in south-east Asia. Of course, it also delivers to Australia, Africa and other parts of the world. Everything from collection by postal vehicles or transfer over post-office counters must work smoothly: in Sweden, 2,200 post offices provide a widely-spread collection network.

Documents — contracts, offers and so on — are part of a vital flow dominated by packages of spare parts, samples, computer accesories and an infinity of other things. Getting them quickly across frontiers — exports on one side, imports on the other — is an important EMS job. Thanks to cooperation with the world's postal and customs services, simplified routines

EMS uses more than 800 flight departures a week in Sweden.

A common sight on Stockholm streets: an EMS vehicle collecting or delivering urgent goods.

and standardised documents save precious minutes. As the need for express freight increases, and competition between different services toughens, EMS must be better, quicker and more reliable to justify its existence.

For example, a tracking-and-tracing computer system is a vital development; it can identify items between collection and destination addresses – 25 Li Yuen Street, Hong Kong; Zutphenseweg 51, Deventer, Holland; 7320 Greenville Avenue, Dallas, USA; or anywhere else on earth.

Radio waves for all

The highest building in Scandinavia, the 155m-high Kaknäs Tower attracts over 30,000 visitors a year, but it was built for Swedish Telecom Radio's domestic and international radio communications.

All radio and TV transmissions to and from Sweden go through its 'switchboard,' as do all radio links for telephone and computer networks, and for mobile telephones and personal-calling devices. These functions define the three principal operational divisions of STR (itself an independent part of Swedish Telecom). Employing 3,000 people, it works unobtrusively, but some of its equipment is very visible: Kaknästornet; the masts at Nacka; the satellite-tracking discs at Tanum on the west coast, and at Ågesta outside Stockholm; and some 50 larger, and 400 smaller, radio and TV transmitting stations in various parts of the country.

STR is thus responsible for three huge domestic and international communication networks: for radio and TV, for telephone and computer communications, and for NMT, *Nordisk Mobil Telefon* service, the world's most widely, and in Sweden the most intensely, used mobile system. In addition there is the personal-seeking system (MBS), also in international use; coastal radio stations in Stockholm, Göteborg and Härnösand, which also operate the international Maritex telex system for maritime users; and these networks' 'tenants:' police forces, various central and local-government services, larger companies and so on.

STR is responsible for the technical side of the domestic flight-navigation and communications networks; its Frequency Administration deals with all national and international aspects of the allocation and use of different radio frequencies. The whole of STR's operations depend to a high degree on international cooperation, for example with the Intelsat and Eutelsat systems, or in planning the future digital mobile-telephone network in Europe, GSM.

STR's high-tech know-how is marketed internationally not just as mobile telephones but as consultative services for, *inter alia*, measuring radiation from antennae in the Vatican – it's hardly possible to get nearer heaven than that.

Stockholm traffic is sometimes turgid, but a mobile telephone keeps you in touch.

An intersection in STR's communications network.

The source of heat and light

Stockholm politicians have always agreed that the capital should be self-supporting in energy, and the responsibility for this has been given to Stockholm Energi.

This is no small job, and with its 420,000 customers, Stockholm Energi is the largest single electricity distributor in Sweden, for the capital consumes 6 TWh electricity (of 135 TWh nationally), divided as follows:

300 high-voltage customers (mainly corporate)	32%
Other corporate customers	39%
Domestic (360,000 households)	25%
The *tunnelbana*	3%
Street lighting	1%

Half domestic consumption is for heating small houses.

To meet these demands, Stockholm Energi has acquired very large resources.

Nuclear power stations at Forsmark and Oskarshamn, part-owned by Stockholm Energi, supply half these needs, and some thermal stations and some ten hydro-electric stations on large rivers in northern and central Sweden supply the rest. Surpluses are sold to other parts of the country.

Consumption keeps rising, but it is increasingly harder to raise production. The time approaches when nuclear-energy generation will begin to be phased out, and for these reasons, Stockholm Energi is trying actively to cut the rate of increase, using advisory services (partly about more effective techniques) and pricing mechanisms to persuade consumers to use electricity more economically. District central-heating, a rational and flexible form of production, uses resources well. Preparations are in hand to incorporate natural gas into the city's energy system, to reduce the vulnerability of dependence on oil.

Traditional gas is still important in Stockholm, and while consumption and numbers of gas-consuming households have decreased, 135,000 gas stoves are in use. Previously, the diminishing trend was encouraged, but plans for natural gas have altered the picture. With natural gas just over the horizon, so to say, it would hardly be wise to scrap the existing gas distribution system.

A better environment is the aim of all these efforts in Stockholm: district central-heating, natural gas, heat-exchange pumps, economical usage. Each contributes to using less oil and to less air-borne pollution.

This is Hammarbyverk, one of Stockholm Energi's most modern plants. Its four large heat-exchangers extract heat from wastewater for use in district-heating systems.

An important part of Stockholm Energi's work is advising on more effective ways to use energy.

Stockholm's largest waterworks, at Norsborg, supplies about 600,000 people with drinking water; it operates 24 hours a day. Its operations, including the flow of water through the works and into the water mains, are run by a central computer unit with substations for different functions.

Venice underground

Stockholm became called 'the Venice of the North' with good reason, being a city founded on a small island – a holm – around which the fresh water of Lake Mälar still discharges into an arm of the Baltic. As Stockholm grew, it spread out over other islands, and is today a city of lakes, canals, streams and sluices. Nowadays there's excellent fishing – seatrout, for example – in the middle of the city, thanks to the largely invisible services of Stockholm Water and Wastewater Works.

The Works now employs some 600 people, and Stockholmers pay about SEK 500m annually for their supplies of first-class drinking water, for unobtrusive domestic and industrial sewage services, and for carefully tended lakes and watercourses – the Works' three main areas of responsibility. Its technology attracts specialists from all over the world.

Much of what interests them is underground; the Henriksdal wastewater treatment plant, for example, is as big as thirty subway stations. It receives sewage water from southern Stockholm, and treats it in a chemical, mechanical and biological computer-controlled process, to remove 90% of its phosphorus and more than 95% of its organic material. A similar plant in

Residual sedimentation is the final step in the purify-ing of wastewater at the Bromma wastewater works to the west of central Stockholm. The biological purifi-cation takes place in the twelve underground basins of the Nockeby facility; operations are controlled by com-puters, so that the entire process may be as effective as possible.

Careful analyses of water are necessary, for it's im-portant to be able to guarantee a high quality of drink-ing water for Stockholmers, and of wastewater ef-fluents into the Baltic. A programme of controls is maintained on the waters of Mälaren, Saltsjön (the arm of the Baltic that reaches into central Stockholm), and the skerries.

Bromma, with stations at Åkeshov and Nocke-by, is amongst the most modern in Europe, for it uses the same techniques, but in conjunction with more sophisticated computer controls. About 85% of the sludge can be used to improve farming lands.

The treated water from Bromma is led to the heat-exchange plant in Solna: the heat goes into the district-heating network, while (from 1989) the cooled water runs through a 7.5 km tunnel bored some 50m below central Stockholm to an arm of the Baltic to the east of the city; previous-ly the outlet was in Mälaren, the source of the city's drinking water.

Stockholm's water mains have a total length of some 5,000 kilometres, and they, like sewage treatment and tunnel building, benefit from constantly renewed technology. There is a method, under development, of maintaining and repairing water mains internally, to avoid the need to dig them up for the purpose. Lakes and watercourses containing excessive quan-tities of fertilizing matter are being treated in a special programme of dredging and cleansing. Bornsjö, a lake to the south west of the city and a reserve source of drinking water, is particular-ly protected. The Works has reached agreement with the farmers of the area to cut back on their use of fertilizers and other agricultural chemi-cals.

So Stockholmers don't see very much of *Stockholm va-verk*, but they do enjoy fine water from their taps and all around the city. Which is really as it should be.

New growth from refuse

Once a week PLM Sellbergs collects refuse from more than 1m Swedes' households; 250,000 households in the Greater Stockholm area yield 145,000 sacks (filled at an average rate of 2.5 kilos a day), making 650 tons to be collected daily by the 450 men on Sellbergs' 215 trucks. Computer-planned routes and strategically chosen re-loading points keep mileage to a minimum. The company collects from many industrial companies; this is most effective when done directly from machines inside factories.

Collection, the most labour-intensive part of the job, can be simplified, but recovery, the next stage, has been transformed by Sellbergs' pioneering work, done with the support of several scientific research institutes.

They and local-government people especially appreciate Sellbergs' BRINI system. Its mechanical sorting and compressing process can turn 21 kilos of refuse into 10 kilos of pellets with a heating value of up to 70% of coal. The first such plant, in Kovik, sells heat to 3,000 households in Bollmora and Tyresö.

Much has been done and much remains to do for, besides heat, refuse can yield compost, metal, new glass, new newsprint (a ton of such paper is equivalent to, and saves, fourteen trees), and methane gas, which is burned in the drying stage of the BRINI system. When used as land fill, refuse can be planted with fast-growing trees and bushes — 'energy woods' in Swedish — to absorb liquid residues and to produce a mass of attractive greenery.

Sellbergs is an old Stockholm company, and Stockholm still provides 50% of its turnover. Among customers further afield are about 50 other Swedish communes, and about 30 local-government districts in Spain!

Fresh greenery and no mistake! A newly-planted 'energy wood' absorbs the liquid residues from the tip and clothes it in attractive foliage.

Refuse is turned in high-energy fuel in a BRINI factory.

The alarm rings here!

For Securitas Teknik there's a clear link between the development of the market and certain well-known trends in the general development of society.

Our oldest customer category is banks, which always need to protect their customers' assets. Here Securitas Teknik clearly leads the market with its alarm equipment for intrusions and TV surveillance, among other things.

The next area is large companies. Their protection against fire has always been vital, and as important today, if not more so, is protection of their large computer facilities from misuse by hackers, and protection of valuable commercial information. Industrial processes themselves are particularly sensitive — a stop in a paper machine, for example, can have devastating

consequences. Industrial customers often ask for intrusion alarms and perhaps more often for means of controlling visitors' access: it's vital to know who is where in an industrial area, and to know at once if some emergency arises. In recent years, public bodies have begun to acquire technical equipment for protective purposes — for example, central government offices, the *riksdag*, hospitals, museums and so on.

Smaller retail units have a rapidly growing need for protection against intrusions; shop-keepers have been unable to afford guards — so they will be seeking technical solutions.

Securitas Teknik offers more than installed equipment, for alarms and the like are nearly always connected to a manned centre, from which measures agreed in advance can be

At Securitas' alarm centre display screens showing automatic alarms from 5,000 customers are kept under scrutiny 24 hours a day. Securitas' personnel alert guards, police or others on duty via telephones or radio.

A 250-strong service cadre makes new installations and maintains 30,000 existing ones in all parts of Sweden.

taken as soon as something happens. An alarm that merely rings is of no use to anyone.

Unlike people, modern aids are on duty day and night, whereas guards are rarely on duty, or on the spot, just when or where some emergency occurs. Electronic detectors, on the other hand, keep an entire area under continuous observation. It naturally saves employees' time to keep several gates and entry points under control from a single, central point. Electronics have made equipment more and more intelligent — an operator is informed not merely that something is on fire, but exactly where the fire is.

In many respects, Sweden is far advanced, especially in taking advantage of technology; in the safety business we use modern electronics and computer techniques to meet contemporary demands. As risks increase in society, so technology will need to meet tough demands to provide a reasonable measure of security in the future.

International in a Swedish perspective

In turnover, numbers of employees and so on Rank Xerox AB forms hardly 1% of the whole Xerox Group – but the Swedish company plays an important role in the Group. Its significance in developmental work is that the Swedish market quickly and readily accepts new, high-technology products.

Rank Xerox established itself in Sweden in 1961, with the modest forecast for the entire Swedish market of 200 copying machines. How wrong can one be? Today there are 120,000 copiers at work in Swedish offices, making 20m paper copies a day! Rank Xerox is a market leader, being in addition one of the country's three largest suppliers of A4 paper.

The copier market is now more or less fully supplied, and Rank Xerox is in the process of moving into a new phase. From having been a straightforward copying-machine company, it is widening its range of products to comprise everything meant by 'document management:' machines, equipment and programs to deal with every aspect of creating, producing, multiplying and distributing documents.

Entering the computer world is a process for pioneers, and Sweden, together primarily with the United States, has enjoyed that role. To an exceptionally high degree, this small country already makes more use of electronics (eg telephones and computers) per capita than any other country. It's natural that tomorrow's helpful machines are being tested here.

During the 1970s, Rank Xerox pioneered word processing in Sweden. In the 1980s, programs are being launched for 'desktop publishing,' or sophisticated graphical work stations and laser printers that work together.

Swedish receptivity for what's new has taken Rank Xerox AB further than other Rank Xerox national companies in diversifying its sales mix.

A well-known Stockholm silhouette seen from the air: the Rank Xerox building in Solna.

Rank Xerox was one of the pioneers of word processing in Sweden, where the company is also launching its desktop-publishing program. This Rank Xerox laser printer is linked online with a mainframe computer at Länsförsäkringsbolagen, an insurance company.

"And how's maintenance going?"

Were there such a thing as a normal management-consultancy case for Idhammar Konsult AB, which specialises in maintenance management, it might be something like the management of a paper mill on the northern Bothnian coast of Sweden (or perhaps on the coast of Tasmania) having a headache over seemingly excessive numbers of breaks in production and turning to Idhammar for relief.

Let us imagine Idhammar beginning an investigation that quickly turns into wide-ranging consultancy, for this imaginary paper mill has a maintenance department, some 200 men strong, that looks after several thousand items of machinery: pumps, motors, valves and so on. Each has to be looked over in the right way at the right time, something that the company's computer people have begun to write a program for. It looks as if costs are going to run to about SEK 20m, so Idhammar proposes the company considers an adaption of its own system, which would cost only a tenth of that.

The management is very well aware of the economic importance of ensuring continuous production, and to be on the safe side the inventory of spare parts has been built up to a

value of some SEK 50m. Idhammar proposes that, with improved planning techniques, this can be substantially reduced. And the proposed inventory control system is introduced.

Among the employees are a number of Tarzan types, who enjoy weekends devoted to successful rescue operations, but they're less keen on routine, preventative maintenance, and constant hunts for symptoms of trouble — the things that make breakdowns and midnight callouts unnecessary. Having met this sort of thing before, Idhammar offers training courses to show how one thing can lead to another (or not), together with a shared view of individuals' areas of responsibility within the company: keeping a 95% level of operation in the whole production facility is the aim. In future, any breakdown will be taken as a sign of malfunctioning maintenance.

The company as a whole doesn't take long to perceive maintenance is better not seen as a cost item, but as a way to increase profitability. At this point Idhammar begins to become a name the company will recall with pleasure, and the Idhammar people can return home to Stockholm.

At a client's office, Idhammar consultants consider how a production system can be refined.

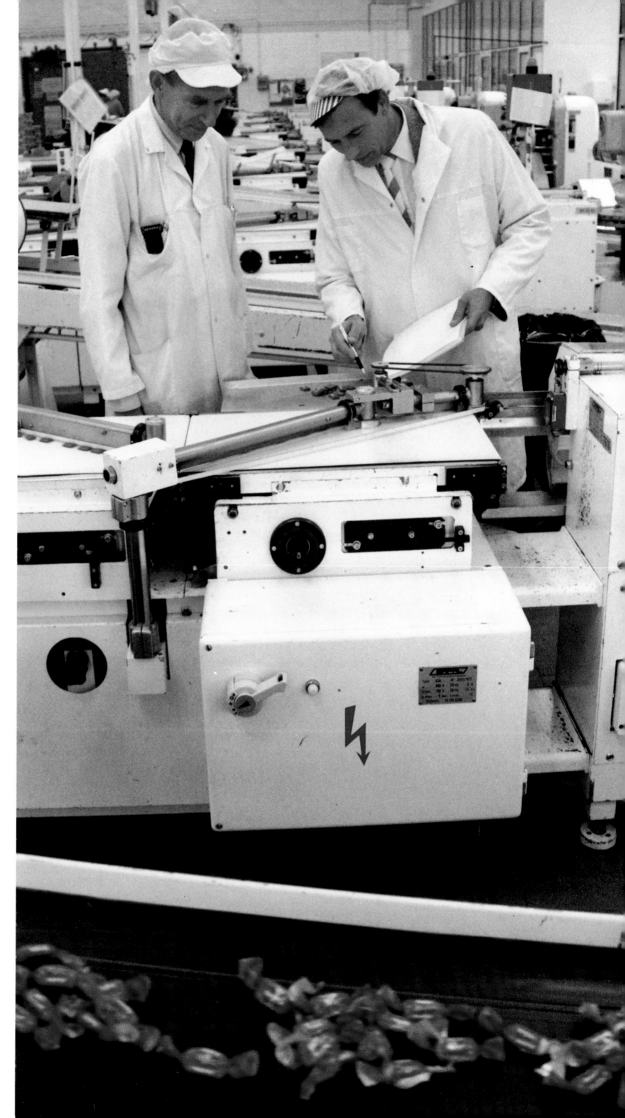

If a single machine or robot goes wrong, it can stop an entire production line. Fieldwork with a client's personnel takes a large part of maintenance consultants' time.

Development continues...

*Each day some 2000
telephone calls are received
and connected in the
'Tower.'*

At Kontorsutveckling's head office at Solna, one finds "the Tower" before the Reception Office. No real tower, it's a landscape office, and the control centre of Kontorsutveckling's communications network with its customers. A computer program helps "flight controllers" to direct each of 2,000 daily phone calls correctly within Kontorsutveckling — to salesmen, operators, programmers, technicians.

At first sight, Kontorsutveckling, which sells systems based on IBM and Apple computers, may seem to be only one of many such companies, but its comprehensive strategy has caused it to expand, while countless other companies have succeeded only briefly.

Kontorsutveckling offers people at work the means to write, calculate, present results and keep track of their work. Its name is down to earth — 'Office Development' — stating plainly what it does. This is unusual in the computer

business, which often bemuses people with super-sophisticated high-tech names and methods. Kontorsutveckling's logo conveys the positive response of a satisfied customer — 'AHA, now I get it!'

The company sells personal computer systems and consulting, training and program packets, and development back-ups, through a chain of offices throughout Sweden, and through subsidiaries in Denmark, Norway and Finland. Technical Systems, a subsidiary, offers advanced CAD/CAM systems for design work, industrial automation, and technical calculations.

The company uses its employees' resources of knowledge and experience, and its suppliers' skills, for the benefit of all concerned, and gives expression to its thoughts about communication in its structures of ownership. In 1988, the Esselte Group became its parent company and

Development of an advanced CAD/ CAM system.

This is the program library, where new programs can be tested.

then added Esselte Datasoft (software and computer ancilliaries) to the group, which also includes a finance company, Nordisk Hyrdata.

Regulating temperatures

Landis & Gyr, on Elektronvägen, was once called Billman-Regulator, and is now the oldest and largest industry in Huddinge. (The name changed in 1987, but Landis & Gyr had become the majority shareholder by 1970.)

Its founder, Stig Billman, built up his company in the 1930s, on automatic controls for central heating systems − technical equipment for effecting correctly regulated indoor climates − in houses, blocks of flats, offices, factories and other buildings.

External developments have often stimulated the company, something that happened first when people began to demand a more even, pleasant temperature in the places where they worked or lived; thus regulators came into general use. A further impulse came from rising energy costs, which made automatics profitable in regulating consumption to meet varying demands during the day and night.

The most drastic changes came as micro-processors came into widespread use; they are as if made to take care of heating and humidity of indoor spaces. Today it's possible to program a computer to look after conditions in buildings that need not be close together.

For example, a single computer regulates the whole of the Stockholm suburb of Skärholmen and saves one fifth or one quarter of energy costs: the whole facility thus paid for itself in less than two years. The same computer can also do a great deal more: receive alarms that something has gone wrong in a lighting circuit for example, or in a lift or an electric lock.

Computer-based equipment enables a building manager to keep several premises under control simultaneously; the work of his employees becomes much more effective. A single caretaker, for example, can lower the temperature in all the schools in a single town, if each is equipped with an intelligent sub-station.

When the company's name changed in 1987, its activities were extended with the creation of its new energy division, which supplies products and services to power generating companies. The division includes Ermi AB in Karlskrona, the largest maker of electricity meters in Scandinavia, and a large cadre of technicians and other specialists.

Through its forty sales and service offices spread over Sweden, the company covers the whole chain of products and services for automatic control and supervision − from electricity meters at power stations to thermostats on individual radiators that ensure the right temperatures in houses, schools and offices at all times.

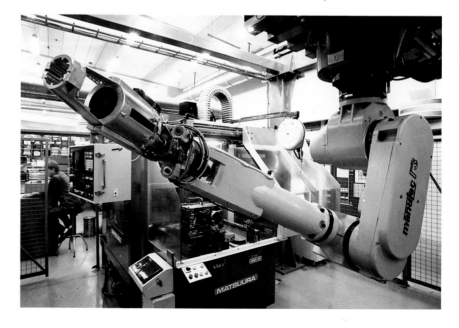

Landis & Gyr is the largest and oldest company in the Stockholm suburb of Huddinge.

Metering equipment under control at a 70kV sub-station.

A robot at work in manufacturing.

Do temperature and humidity agree? Landis & Gyr's facilities for control of internal climates at the Electrum electronic centre at Kista are given a final adjustment.

A DYNAMIC CENTRE:
Stockholm as a building site
– what activity!

Building in progress – cranes, concrete trucks, scaffolding, re-directed traffic and the rest of it – characterises Stockholm of the 1980s, and so much new work has begun in the last few years that politicians have even thought it necessary to put the brakes on a bit. Work is in progress almost everywhere, from the inner city out to the suburbs.

The motorway from the north, for example, is fringed with new complexes of dwellings, offices and industrial premises: around Arlanda, at the GLG-Center in Upplands Väsby, in Kista (the Silicon Valley of Sweden), at the new SAS headquarters in Solna.

Rail travellers arrive almost in the middle of the construction site, over the tracks, of the Vasaterminal: one of the biggest glazed roofs in the world will cover a bus terminal, the Stockholm World Trade Center and a virtual district of office premises. In much the same way, work costing some SEK 3,500m is proceeding over the railway on the South Side – from the city centre it's the rocky outcrop on the southern skyline. This new district of dwellings and offices will further exemplify how Stockholm makes the best use of its limited resources of land.

Unlike many other international cities, Stockholm has said No to skyscrapers, wanting to keep her traditional skyline of churches and the classical City Hall intact as far as possible. But there are exceptions, and the most prominent is also on the South Side.

The Stockholm Globe Arena, which will be the largest spherical building in the world, is taking form in time for the 1989 Ice-Hockey World Championships. Hotels, offices and shopping centres are being built around it, at a cost of nearly SEK 2,000m.

While computer technology has its centre in Kista, doctors and biotechnologists are gathered in the area around the big hospital in Huddinge. New scientific centres, a new university, and a new domestic airport are being planned here. Energy technology will acquire a centre of its own in Skrubba.

New urban districts are being built, and old ones saved, with less demolition and more renovation of old houses: every posssible square metre of their floor space is being used. Attics, once used only for storage, are being turned into attractive apartments.

As in most large cities, commercial premises in inner Stockholm have grown enormously, from 8m square metres in 1950 to 13.5m in 1985, an increase of nearly 70%. Dwelling areas have increased very much less, from 9.2m in 1950 to 10.1 in 1985, an increase of about 10%.

In the outer areas, by contrast, dwelling areas have grown very much faster in the past few decades, but efforts are being made now – in the form, among others, of new office and industrial parks, as at Kista – to locate new places of work near dwelling areas.

On the national-political level efforts are made to balance the powerful growth of the region, which still allures many. It's been reckoned that an additional 3m square metres of office space will come into use during the next five years, equivalent to projects costing SEK 30,000 to 40,000m.

A city of islands and holms must make the best use of all its land. Building is in progress over the Central Station tracks of offices, a bus terminal, the Stockholm World Trade Center, and much else.

On the South Side, a new city centre is under construction around the railway station, where architects are merging new buildings with the old to create a new housing environment.

Architects who found a winning model

FFNS Gruppen AB, a limited company offering a full range of professional architectural services, was the first Swedish company of this sort to be introduced on the Stockholm Stock Exchange. This was no coincidence, although the professional tradition is of predominately small companies, often built up around a central, founding figure, for this revolutionary possibility was inherent in its founding. At the end of the 1950s, four architects (their names had the initials F F N & S) decided to use this legal form for their professional ambitions, a limited company to be run on strict business lines.

Step by step the group has reached a position in which a market quotation was the natural next step. With 20 offices in Sweden, and with nearly half its 400 employees working in the Stockholm office, FFNS is by far the largest architects' company in Sweden; it has the stability needed by a company with quoted shares.

The architect's professional role calls for competence in many areas: form and aesthetics, behaviour, technology, economics, planning, leading and managing a project. More and more often, those commissioning a building require the architect – or someone else – to assume total responsibility for the job. Only a relatively large company can maintain in-house expertise in every area affected by a large building project. At its head office, FFNS has many functional units: for project management, information technology using photography, computer graphics, model-building and copying. There are, too, specialists in interior-design, land, landscaping and gardening.

Its size and economic stability have also allowed FFNS to take a professional lead in developing modern techniques, including computers, of course, which have freed much time for the essence of an architect's job, the creative work.

FFNS is certainly large but no architectural factory: on the contrary, the architects who work in the company share no common style, but subscribe to the same principle of 'carefully achieved quality for everyday use.' This has not hindered constant competition for spearhead commissions: what is thought exclusive and extreme today can be the model for tomorrow's accepted style.

FFNS has now established itself in London – a world in itself, and a window on the world– where the company will follow its Swedish customers as they establish themselves outside Sweden.

A new design in old surroundings in the centre of Stockholm.

Work-in-progress in the new district on the South Side, where FFNS has designed 480 dwellings.

What do you think of the model? It's for a new office project in Zug, in Switzerland.

6 M³ K30 No: 18!

"6 cubic metres K30, 18, specially liquid, delivery by rotary pump 0820 hours." Such was one of a thousand orders received at the central order office of Betongindustri on a quite ordinary day: it was for concrete for a new liftshaft in an old building.

The mix was one of hundreds stored in the computer, and available at a moment: decoded, this one means durability of class K30, maximum stone size of 18mm, fluid enough to be pumped up into the forms.

As usual, timing was vital. Concrete must be used fresh, within an hour of being mixed, for what happens otherwise is all too easy to imagine. Today, mixing and distribution is an advanced process industry with high demands for precision and planning — a matter of grams and minutes!

In the Stockholm area Betongindustri has led the market, and possessed resources for the entire production chain, for many years:
● large gravel pits on islands in Mälaren, with boat links to centrally located depots in the city; (the Jehanders subsidiary.)
● concrete-mixing plants, delivery trucks, ancilliary equipment, for example for heating in winter; (the parent company and two subsidiaries, Termater and BSL Maskin.)
● manufacture and erection of concrete elements; (Strängbetong.)

● production facilities for wholly new factories to modernisation of older premises; (another subsidiary, Röbäcks Mekaniska.)

Concrete need not be grey or clumsy, but can have almost any colour or form, particularly if elements are used. Architects have begun to appreciate this, not least in building office premises and hotels. A fruitful interplay between architects, building contractors and makers of concrete elements, has created new forms and structures. Concrete is on the way to conquering new markets.

Pumps over the whole world

In 1939, when Börje Kristenson, an engineer of the classical school — a designer, inventor and workshop operator all in one — founded a company with a good friend, he was not to know that, by the 1980s, it would be one of the first in the world for submersible pumps for the building and mining industries, nor that it would be called Grindex.

It began life by producing spark plugs, gaskets, brake shoes and many other things for the automobile trade, but its development into present-day Grindex would be anything but simple. It survived during WW2 thanks to Börje Kristenson's engineering talents: its production switched into firing mechanisms for Swedish defense forces' needs and switched again in 1945, when military stores were stocked for many years' needs. The company then returned to the automobile trade, with vacuum brakes for vehicles and trailers. A later product was a grinding machine (which gave the company a name) for engineering workshops and, later again, grinding machines for mining drills.

Contact with the mining industry, and visits to mines, where water is always a problem, laid the foundation for Grindex as it is known today. By the early 1960s Grindex introduced a wholly submersible pump. It proved a great success, and while its basic design has endured, its technical development has continued without a break. The latest models incorporate the ECONOMATIC electronic control unit: it supervises pumps to ensure none runs when there is too little water to pump. Wear-and-tear and energy consumption is greatly reduced in this way.

The market needs not just effective pumps, but also swift response to customers' needs and rapid service. Grindex met this demand by building up comprehensive retail, service and rental networks. In Sweden Grindex pumps can be bought and serviced at more than fifty locations, or hired from many of the plant-hire companies in the country.

More than 80% of Grindex' products are exported, so it's easy to understand the company has a very good position on the international market. Grindex pumps are to be found in more than 70 countries, from Iceland to Fiji; they've helped people keep dry footed on a number of internationally known building sites — for example, the Thames barrage downstream from the City of London, the underground railway system in Hong Kong, the Agoyan hydro-electric dam in Equador, the nuclear power station at Oskarshamn, and the enormous Majes irrigation project in Peru.

A good pump must pump water but not try to pump air. Here a motor housing and its gaskets are under inspection.

What will be Stockholm's biggest new tourist attraction, the Wasa Museum, faces the same problem as that of most other building sites — rising water. And solves it in the same way, with Grindex pumps.

The right man in the right place

On the motorway between Stockholm and Arlanda, you can't fail to notice GLG Center, the largest privately-owned company center in Sweden, just at the point where Upplands Väsby begins.

Among 130 companies, there are Cederroths, Norsk Data, ICL and many others, and their 2,000 or more employees. And, in fact, while you're reading this they have probably employed a few more people and perhaps some more companies have moved in.

In the early 1970s, cows were grazing here when Lars Gullstedt came looking for an industrial site. He had with him experience from his childhood on a farm near Närpes, a small town on the Bothnian coast of Finland, and from work in Sweden — a carpenter in his 20s, a building contractor in his 30s. When one of his

customers went bankrupt, his company only just managed to survive: Lars Gullstedt had learnt a lesson — in future he would build for himself, so that he should have real security behind him.

He wanted a site on the E4 between Stockholm and Arlanda, and found first one, then eight more, in Upplands Väsby, then mostly pasture and potato fields. He built his own sewage works, drilled wells, instigated exits from the motorway (and financed them principally himself), where there is now a sign pointing to GLG Center. Large and small companies have been attracted there, the company itself grows, Lars Gullstedt builds new premises all the time, and new tenants are always to be found.

By 1987 200,000 square metres of floor space were in use, with a further 20,000 planned or

under construction. So GLG Center has become a living centre for companies, with its Service Center, conference and leisure facilties, restaurants, banks, travel agencies, shops, lawyers' and auditors' offices.

By chance, Lars Gullstedt bought a company, Metall-Teknik, which was the country's principal maker of self-service entries, exits and shopping-trolley automats. He complemented it with Edströms Sweden (car interiors) in GLG Center, and Borgströms (interiors for service vehicles) in Kilafors. He acquired his own finance company, Ergu Finans and bought an interest in the consulting company Xellence.

The Gullstedt Group grows apace in the new Service Center. It has 2,000 square metres of marble, and the area that started with relatively sparsely furnished industrial premises now contains a luxurious office complex. It's only the first.

FACING THE 21ST CENTURY

By the year 2000, Stockholm will have come to be more than the capital of Sweden.

The region has the best chance of any in Sweden of developing a creative business life that can maintain its position in an international competition that hardens all the time.

Besides a rich, many-facetted cultural life, the region can give its inhabitants a unique environment to live in, with open country waiting undisturbed at *tunnelbana* distance from the inner city.

By the end of the century, Stockholm can be a vital part of an international network and the motor for the development of the whole of Sweden.

But will this be at the price of weakening other parts of the country, of unbalancing Sweden? Would rapid growth of the region itself worsen its existing imbalance between a favoured north and an unfavoured south? Are individuals favoured by what favours industry, commerce and science?

Seven people, with power to influence the region in different ways, try here to envisage Stockholm in 2000.

INGELA THALÉN

Appointed Minister of Labour in autumn 1987, Ingela Thalén had been Chairperson of the Commune Council in Järfälla for five years before this not unexpected elevation to national political responsibility within the Social Democratic Party. While still in Järfälla, she had put the commune's economy to rights, and could pride herself on the fact that a number of high-tech companies had located to Järfälla, which lies close to both the motorways running west (E18) and north (E4) from Stockholm.

She began by stating that had forecasts from the 1960s and 1970s been correct, by 1987 Järfälla would have reached a population of some 90,000, instead of its present 56,000; she expressed her belief that it will have hardly risen above 60,000 by the end of the century.

"We decided in principle not to build on our large green area to the east."

She admitted many people may see this as luxury, when the housing queue within the commune contains 4,000 names, of which 2,500 are those of young people. "But if we and our children are to live well in the Stockholm area, we must look after the areas of open country that still exist close to the city."

As in Haninge, 20,000 people in the commune commute to jobs outside it, and shortening commuting times was her goal in Järfälla, as it is Westin's in Haninge (see p. 129). Ideally, this would be done by attracting more sound companies to Järfälla or near it." "Better communications and links between the main lines of communication are also necessary."

Järfälla offers good industrial areas and closeness to good road communications, not least to Arlanda, which is becoming a new power centre in the industrial development of the region. Thalén considered that Stockholm must be allowed to expand, to be the motor in a refined technical development, from which the whole country can benefit, and that Sweden has exportable knowledge in areas such as health care, administration and organisation. She expressed her belief that industry and commerce around the whole of Mälaren possess great possibilities for development, if communications are developed faster. High-speed trains between Stockholm and towns such as Örebro and Västerås would create new possibilities for business and regional creators of the society of the future.

She said she wanted Stockholm, by 2000, to be a town that, foremost, had preserved the waters of Mälaren, and developed itself into a living environment, rich in things to do and enjoy even after office-closing hours.

"By all means, build high-rise buildings in the middle of Stockholm and let people move in to the centre. Create cafés, movement and the possibility of being together without thoughts of prestige. This is also the problem for Järfälla and most of the other communes around Stockholm. We must open society during evenings and at weekends."

Ingela Thalén, appointed Minister of Labour in autumn 1987, had been Chairperson of the Commune Council in Järfälla, a Stockholm suburb.

Viksjö School, Järfälla, tries to ensure all pupils get to learn about computers.

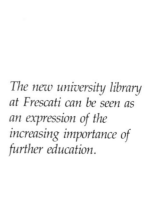

The new university library at Frescati can be seen as an expression of the increasing importance of further education.

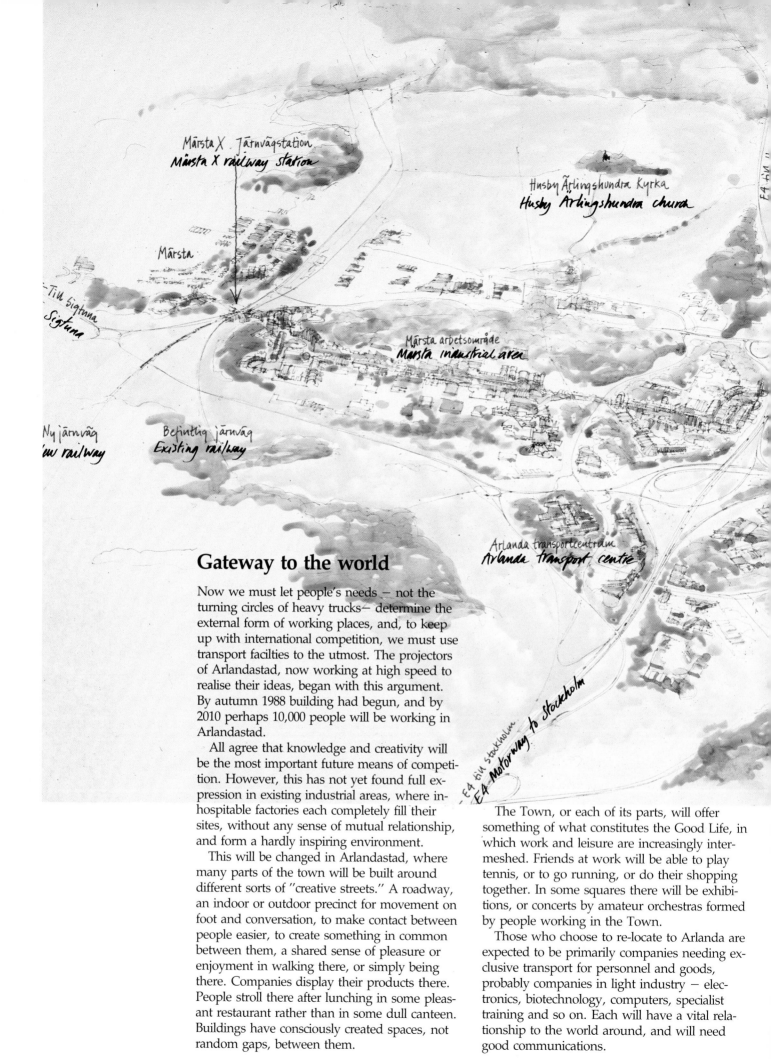

Mårsta X Järnvägstation
Mårsta X railway station

Husby Ärlingshundra Kyrka
Husby Ärlingshundra church

Mårsta

Till Sigtuna
Sigtuna

Mårsta arbetsområde
Mårsta industrial area

Ny järnväg
'ew railway

Befintlig järnväg
Existing railway

Arlanda transportcentrum
Arlanda transport centre

E4 till stockholm
E4 Motorway to stockholm

Gateway to the world

Now we must let people's needs — not the turning circles of heavy trucks— determine the external form of working places, and, to keep up with international competition, we must use transport facilties to the utmost. The projectors of Arlandastad, now working at high speed to realise their ideas, began with this argument. By autumn 1988 building had begun, and by 2010 perhaps 10,000 people will be working in Arlandastad.

All agree that knowledge and creativity will be the most important future means of competition. However, this has not yet found full expression in existing industrial areas, where inhospitable factories each completely fill their sites, without any sense of mutual relationship, and form a hardly inspiring environment.

This will be changed in Arlandastad, where many parts of the town will be built around different sorts of "creative streets." A roadway, an indoor or outdoor precinct for movement on foot and conversation, to make contact between people easier, to create something in common between them, a shared sense of pleasure or enjoyment in walking there, or simply being there. Companies display their products there. People stroll there after lunching in some pleasant restaurant rather than in some dull canteen. Buildings have consciously created spaces, not random gaps, between them.

The Town, or each of its parts, will offer something of what constitutes the Good Life, in which work and leisure are increasingly intermeshed. Friends at work will be able to play tennis, or to go running, or do their shopping together. In some squares there will be exhibitions, or concerts by amateur orchestras formed by people working in the Town.

Those who choose to re-locate to Arlanda are expected to be primarily companies needing exclusive transport for personnel and goods, probably companies in light industry — electronics, biotechnology, computers, specialist training and so on. Each will have a vital relationship to the world around, and will need good communications.

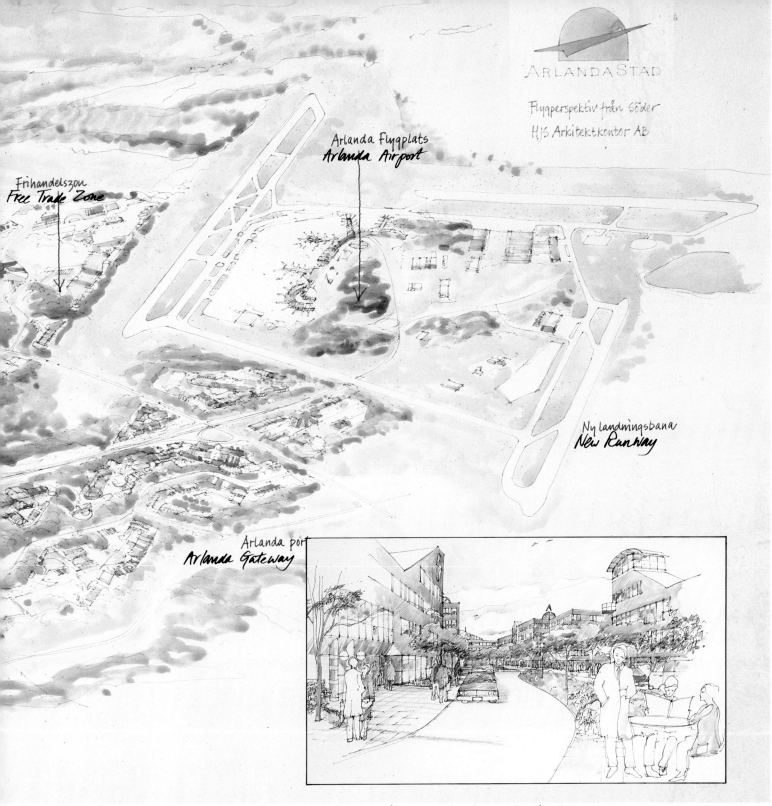

Frihandelszon
Free Trade Zone

Arlanda Flygplats
Arlanda Airport

Ny landningsbana
New Runway

Arlanda port
Arlanda Gateway

ArlandaStad

Flygperspektiv från söder
HJS Arkitektkontor AB

Twelve million passengers a year currently pass through Arlanda, and it's reckoned their numbers will double within twenty years. Sweden's international contacts will increase more and more in what, in a long-term perspective, will perhaps come to be called the United World. For regional contacts there are access to both the main northern line of the railway and the E4 motorway with its attractive exhibition possibilities.

No-one can say today exactly how Arlandastad will look in the future. Planning and extensions go on continuously, with active participation from the established companies.

The business concept for Arlandastad is to create an international aesthetic and enlivening environment for companies, in a region that is the "Door to Scandinavia," that can develop people, and their products, companies and markets.

Development can seem slow – if one's in the lead

A microcircuit chip the size of your little finger nail –, 6 mm×6 mm, or a quarter of an inch either way – accomodates 100,000 transistors, the heart of a modern computer. Had the 1950s state of the art been used instead, the computer would have been as big as the Palace and consumed the output of a medium-sized power station.

Semi-conductor techniques have been simply essential to electronics' progress, and Hafo has been in the lead all the time. The heart pacemaker was the breakthrough, for it made quite clear the special features of micro-electronics are their minute size and usage of energy, their great reliability. Once operated into the human body, a pacemaker must work perfectly for the ten-year lifetime of its battery, for it is literally vital that it never misses a beat.

Hafo has also staked a claim on some other niches: one is optocomponents for electronics in telecommunications, another is over-voltage protection for electronics in telephones and other areas, a third is microcircuits for space technology, in which one parameter is ability to withstand cosmic radiation.

Hafo's testing facilities check its own bought-in components, which number about 30m a year, and are available to the entire Swedish electronics industry. Hafo's general activities,

however, are still based on microcircuit chips, and while makers compete fiercely, Hafo has chosen to specialise in chips for specific applications – tailor-made, as one might say, in the Extra-Small range. All current forecasts suggest the whole industry will be doing this during the 1990s, once designers have achieved their expected breakthrough, which people at Hafo are waiting for, a little impatiently.

The technology exists, and is in fact easy to learn, for a computer system – MOSart – can search very quickly through a library of cells to find the ones needed for some specific microcircuit design. Hafo believes it can demonstrate the economic advantages of this method and is trying to persuade the electronics industry, by means of a comprehensive information campaign, to hurry on the breakthrough.

Silicon chips with microcircuits on their way into the high-temperature kiln for diffusion.

Interior view of HAFO's Design Center, heart of development of microcircuits.

123

JAN-ÅKE GUSTAFSSON
Professor in Medical Nutrition at Huddinge Hospital, and Managing Director of the Center for Life Sciences, the heart of a planned cooperation between pure and clinical research, and industry, at Huddinge Hospital. Also active in the formation of the genetics company called KaroBio.

"For Swedish academic and industrial life, holding an international front level in the life sciences is of the utmost importance. The question's not if but how to invest."

"Nowadays, almost all medical research needs genetic technology, and so do the medical-drug and other industries. This type of competence is a spearhead. Since 1984, we've had much support from the county administration for a life-sciences center, where the eternal research flame burns, with contacts with clinical work, and pure and straightforwardly commercial research.

Professor Jan Åke Gustafsson and colleagues.

A model of Novum, at the regional planning office. The Centre for Life Sciences is being built up by industry, the Karolinska Institute, and the county administration. The plans for the region include a university, an airport, and attractive dwelling areas.

"Our center is associated with KaroBio and the Institute for Medical Nutrition. The former is a research-intensive life-sciences company Astra and Pharmacia could use, instead of looking abroad for further development. Politicians are still interested in this investment at the hospital — it would give the Karolinska Institution a new, southern focus.

"This form of regional planning isn't questioned by anyone. All at once, many things make sense: commuter and long-distance train services, an airport at Tullinge, a 'village' for research and a hotel for researchers, and leisure facilities."

Some orthodox researchers may dislike cooperation with industry, but he's not one of them.

"It increases creativity and strengthens one's scientific muscle. In this way we'd have better chances to retain our best researchers in Sweden. The state alone can never provide the resources needed for us to remain internationally competitive."

HARRY SCHEIN
Chairman of the boards of the Swedish Investment Bank, and of the Swedish Broadcasting Corporation, Schein began his public career in the early 1960s, when he drafted a scheme for a Swedish film institute, which came into being in 1963. He was a friend and advisor to Olof Palme and is also a controversial Social Democratic intellectual. He came to Stockholm in his teens, a refugee from another big city, Vienna.

"My starting point is that almost all forecasts go wrong. We look for changes which never occur, while we seldom succeed in forecasting the big changes.

"According to forecasts ten years ago we would now have offices without paper, in a society without money in the form of notes and coins. Nothing of the sort! It's become more and more difficult to see what will happen, because the very speed of changes has become so much greater, while at the same time our whole existence has been internationalised."

According to Schein, Sweden's ambition — to maintain an inner balance in this large country with a small population — is one of its problems.

"There's a spontaneous, natural pressure from a number of activities and people who all want to come to Stockholm. Then national politicians try to push in the opposite direction, to move as many activities as possible out into the country. It's possible this a Don Quixote enterprise." Schein notes the Soviet Union, which has other, unSwedish means at its disposal, hasn't prevented enormous population growth in Moscow: "It's almost compulsory for other Soviet citizens to have a visa for Moscow."

Schein believes the next few years will make heavy demands on Swedish industry, which at present has trouble in attracting young, well-educated workers.

"The nature of industrial work must be changed. The trade-union movement must accept that artificial boundaries between blue-collar and white-collar workers have begun to shift."

According to Schein, by 2000 Stockholm will still face two of today's most pressing economic problems: a shrinking industrial sector, for which a service sector cannot compensate, and a wage-and-salary-fixing mechanism that gives too much room to irresponsible parties on the labour market.

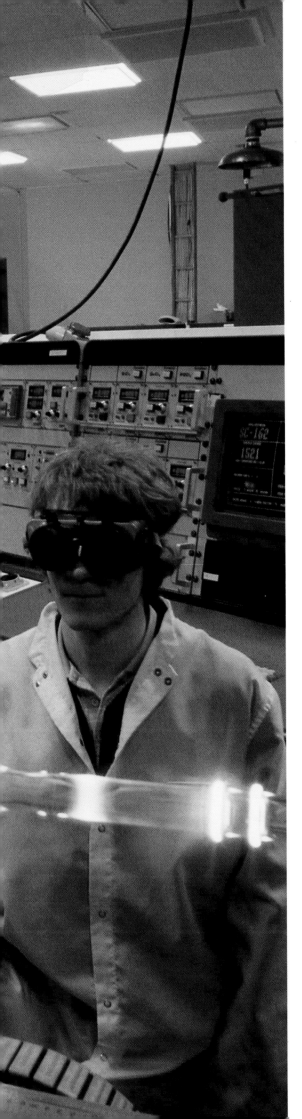

PETER WEISSGLAS
*Director of the Institute for Microwave Technology.
One of the moving spirits behind Electrum in Kista, a
centre for research and education in electronics and
computing science. A keen proponent of a deeper
cooperation between academic research and industry
and not least between education and the business
world.*

Big things are happening in Kista. A suburb
north of Stockholm has developed into a centre
for the Swedish electronics and computing industry, where 25,000 people will soon be working. Fifteen years ago there was virtually nothing here.

The Kista area is a consequence of a common
employment of resources by Stockholm, institutes of further education, and business, to
give Sweden more competent researchers,
competitive ideas for products and so a better
position on the world market. Just back from a
meeting where Volvo and Saab discussed cooperation over future electronics in the car industry, Weissglas says: "I believe we will be seeing
more and more large-scale projects in which industries work together."

"International cooperation is a dimension
that's becoming more and more important. It's
no longer a matter of contacts between researchers but long-term organised joint direction.

"Wholly new networks are being built up between companies and countries, that result in
mergers and cooperation. Everything is developing towards 'big science,' in which demands and prices for apparatus increase rapidly, as do demands for all the peripheral areas of
knowledge you must be able to draw in.

"In Kista we have, among other jobs, that of
helping industry find tomorrow's technology.
Our sights are set eight to ten years into the
future, and our work is geared for results re-
lated to the needs we see before us.

"Today, Kista is the only area in Sweden that
possesses all the preconditions for becoming a
really modern industrial centre. From Kista to
the town of Arlanda, on the Stockholm-Uppsa-
la axis, a really dynamic area is coming into
existence. Such condensations contain so many
positive coordination effects.

"We have the people, we have the communications, we have the resources for education
and training. Not only Stockholm, but the
whole of Sweden, can be developed here."

*Making optical fibres at
Ericsson's.*

STAFFAN BURENSTAM LINDER
*Professor of International Economics at the Stockholm
School of Economics. Minister of Trade in two non-
socialist administrations and for many years spokes-
man for the Moderate (conservative) Party on international economics.*

"Stockholm should be a successful business
centre. We're a bit peripheral but electronics
and airplanes make us less so. For people of the
future closeness to nature will come to mean
more for conditions of living. Skiing, picking
mushrooms and woodland fungi, skating, and
ten minutes' journeys to work give many of us
interesting advantages.

"But the degree of our success depends on
which economic policy we get, and that's not
provided by God. Clean air does not overcome
every degree of taxation. And measures of
socialisation, and regulations, stifle energy, so
may we be preserved from such things if we
don't want Stockholm to become a regional-
political problem in the larger world.

"So a high-class education system is needed,
in which one dares to put a premium on, and to
acknowledge, quality. Education is becoming
all the more important for the future. The world
is becoming larger and larger, in that more and
more successful countries are entering the
scene. If one wishes to be remarked amongst
them one must be well educated.

"The Stockholm School of Economics is the
only private institute of higher education in
Sweden. I believe we'd have a better education
system with more such private institutions
competing with one another, with governing
boards knowing their schools' futures de-
pended on the degree of their engagement.

"Getting foreign researchers here is easy, but
it's easiest in late spring and for short periods
before taxes begin to bite. This says something
about our competitive position."

*Watersports on Riddar-
fjärden, central
Stockholm.*

GUNNAR WESTIN

As Director of local-government services in Haninge commune, and its highest-ranking employee, Westin is considered by many to be something of a visionary or ideologist for local-government politicians in Södertörn, the southern part of the Greater Stockholm region. Compared with the northern part, Södertörn is less well served with communications and roads, less favoured industrially, and less attractive to live in.

"We're moving into a post-industrial society which will be dominated by high-tech and knowledge companies, and it's important to acknowledge that, and to examine what it's going to mean in general terms. We must do this in a wide, international perspective, for if we don't Sweden risks becoming a backwater. We do certainly need the drive a big urban region like Stockholm can give, but the region itself must be balanced. Its present long-standing imbalance between north and south is the sort of segregation that shouldn't exist in a well-developed, democratic society.

To Westin, the region south of Stockholm clearly must have its own domestic airport, at Tullinge, and Haninge, with 60,000 inhabitants of whom 20,000 work outside the commune,

must have a motorway link with the E4, the motorway south from Stockholm. More people must be closer to their places of work, for shorter journeys mean an improvement in the quality of their lives: achieving this before the end of the century is one of the main goals he's set himself.

"We're struggling against a tradition that causes everything at all respectable — including state administrative bodies — to be located to the north of the capital." He hopes more long-sighted companies will appreciate the advantages of southern Stockholm, and that Huddinge Hospital will be developed into a centre primarily for biotechnical research and education. Haninge is a suburb that's now shed its 1970s' reputation of having social problems, but he admits it'll take some time before city-centre yuppies in consulting and financial companies leave their owner-occupied apartments for this southern suburb.

"We're not aiming at that, though. We'd like there to be a mixed population — young and old, many different sorts of job. Of the immigrant 10% of the population we have great hopes that they will give a richer and more colourful life to the community.

Doctors' training is being decentralised: this is from Sollentuna Hospital.

Home-care unit at work.

Thanks to a local campaign, more than 3,000 kids in Sollentuna now sport bike helmets.

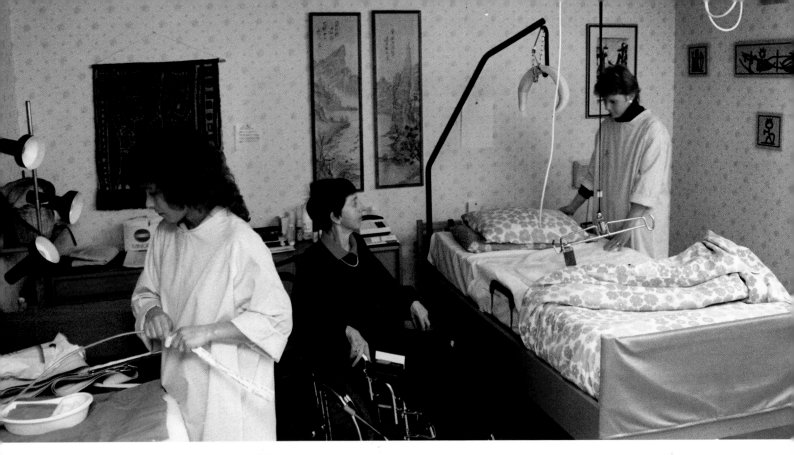

A new approach

The county administration of Stockholm is making an effort to achieve decentralisation and open health-care. In March 1986, under the name of 'A New Approach,' the considerable work of re-organising the county administration was begun. Responsibility and powers were to be transfered to the basic administrative areas, so as to make better use of the resources of knowledge and personal commitment among the personnel.

Open health care in local health-care centres has been greatly extended since the 1970s, and the positive effects of an extended primary-care service in large urban areas have been documented in a number of studies.

The personnel works in work teams that serve a given geographical area, so as to get to know the people there more thoroughly, one of the aims being that people should get the health care they need at home, rather than in a hospital. Questions of this sort are urgent matters for research, and its results can be of great importance in the future.

The significance of the environment and individuals' social situations for their health are attracting more and more attention. Information about health and diet are already part of health-care centres' work. Emergency surgeons visit schools in the county to give information about the consequences of traffic accidents and other forms of violence. In Sollentuna, a northern suburb of Stockholm, a campaign has been carried on to persuade kids to use bike helmets. The most important health-care work, however, may be that carried out by voluntary associations, which together cover half the population of the county.

TORD CEWÉ

Now Head of the Environmental Department of the country of Stockholm, Céwe was formerly a national civil servant and a specialist in environmental matters during three political administrations. He is now responsible for ensuring environmental interests are taken account of in all phases of planning work in the Greater Stockholm area.

According to Céwe, while building new dwellings will put great pressure on land use in the Greater Stockholm area, the development of traffic is a greater threat to nature and the environment.

"A new idea for communications for the Stockholm region must evolve before the end of the century. The city on the water is charming but makes for great difficulties in finding solutions for traffic which meet the demands of a large modern city.

"And the planners are doing their utmost to find a way to link the electronics-computer triangle around Kista in the north with what can become a biotechnical triangle round Huddinge Hospital in the south. A motorway extension to the west, Kungshattsled, has priority but an extension to the east, Österled, is not ruled out. It'll be a four-lane, elevated construction with exits and tunnels, taking traffic from Nacka through a tunnel beneath Saltsjön (the arm of the Baltic which extends into the centre of Stockholm) and the southern part of Djurgården, up to the area by Frihamnen, and then through another tunnel beneath Lilljanskogen to Hjorthagen and so up to Roslagstull."

Céwe is disturbed. He feels disturbed by the falling pH values in the soil around Stockholm that tests have revealed. "If the ground sickens, the woods and forests will decline just as quickly." The struggle against emissions of sulphur has been relatively successful in Greater Stockholm in the last twenty years, but dealing with motor-driven vehicles has shown itself to be more difficult to master than dealing with industry.

"More traffic on rail systems — both tramways and express trains — can be an alternative for the future. The internal-combustion engine should not be taken for granted as the foremost means of propulsion in Stockholm traffic by 2000. Thoughts of forbidding private usage of motor transport in the city centre aren't dead but politically difficult. On the other hand, it wouldn't surprise me if some form of toll were introduced before the end of the century, in order to decrease travel by car, and thus emissions, in the inner city."

To preserve Mälaren, the source of drinking water for Stockholmers, a tunnel is now being dug, for completion during the 1990s, right under the capital from the sewage works in Bromma/Åkerhov via Sundbyberg to lead effluents out into Saltsjön. Otherwise, one of the major environmental questions for the 1990s is the Baltic. The nitrogen content of sewage discharges must decrease drastically if the Baltic is not forced to accept more than it can bear. This can require very large investments in new and improved sewage works. Even so, Céwe admits that, in Stockholm, he has a much easier job as a conservator of the environment than colleagues in the other large cities in Europe.

"Most people know that we are caring for unique resources. The care of nature is a part of the Swedish national character, a popular movement. It is not enough to maintain our position up to 2000. Quite simply, we must be better, for if we are not we shall have made a mess of things."

Small-boat harbour at Näsbyviken. The apartment blocks in the background are those of Täby Centrum.

*Enskededalen has an
urban character, while the
houses in Upplands Väsby
(left) are almost idyllically
rural. Terrace houses in
Vårby.*

A town to live in

Buildings from the 1960s and 1970s have been criticized for their over-large scale and their architectural monotony. Work in recent years has been characterised by new thinking in planning and formal language.

*A spaceship has landed.
The Stockholm Globe
Arena is planned for
completion in time for the
1989 World Cup in ice
hockey.*

If approaching Stockholm by train from the south, keep a sharp lookout a few minutes before arrival: to the left after the viaduct over Årstaviken lies the area of small-gardens-with-little-houses, or koloniområde, of Tantolunden. The twin towers in the background are those of Högalid church.

"On a fine Thursday morning in July many people streamed past Riddarholms church to where the steamers lay. Everyone hastened to **Yngve Frej** and rushed over the gangway as quick as they could, for the time of sailing had already passed, and the captain had already ordered " 'All visitors ashore.' "

This is the opening passage of Carl Jonas Love Almqvist's **Det går an** (It's perhaps alright), a short story published in 1838. Its theme — the superiority of free love over formal marriage — was controversial at the time, but no-one has ever argued with Almqvist's accurate description, valid still today, of the summer charms of the waters surrounding Stockholm.

Facts about Stockholm

Traditionally, Stockholm was founded as a town in the mid13th century by Birger Jarl ('Earl Birger'); the name is first recorded in 1252. Effectively the capital of Sweden before the end of the 16th century, the city became the formal capital in 1634. Its oldest surviving buildings lie in the Old Town and date from the late 13th century: Storkyrkan ('Great Church') and Riddarholmskyrkan ('Knights' Holm Church'). Its loftiest structure is the 20th century Kaknäs transmitting tower; it's 155m high and three or four kilometres east of central Stockholm.

The Old Town, the City and the Region of Stockholm

What is now called the Old Town (Gamla Stan) occupies the location of the historical capital. It was also called the Town Between the Bridges, from the bridges over the waters of Lake Mälar that ran out to the Baltic around the holms or islands on which the town grew up. The City of Stockholm is the name given to the present administrative unit, *Stockholms kommun*. The region of Stockholm, or Greater Stockholm, comprises twentytwo communes, including that of Stockholm.

Area population

The City has an area of 216 sq.km. (of which 19% is water), and the region an area of about 4,900 sq.m. (30% water). Its 1987 population is, in brief, as follows:

Population	Stockholm	All Sweden
The city	663,000	8%
The region	1,450,000	17%
In employment	344,000	4,269,000
	%	%
− agriculture & forestry	4	−
− manufacturing	13	24
− construction	4	6
− trade	18	14
− banking & insurance	15	8
− transport	9	7
− public administration	41	37
	100%	100%
Employment among married women	86%	83%
Unemployment among men	2%	3%
Unemployment among women	1%	3%

The climate & the seasons

The mean temperature in Stockholm varies between 3°C (26°F) in January and +18°C (64°F) in July. Comparative figures for some other capitals are:

London	+5°C/41°F	+18°C/64°F
New York	+1°C/34°F	+25°C/77°F
Madrid	+4°C/40°F	+24°C/75°F
Paris	+3°C/37°F	+19°C/66°F

Public buildings, the arts, museums & sport Stockholm

Public buildings

The Palace, Royal Treasury & Royal Armoury Old Town. Ceremonial carriages, regalia. (Information by telephone: 7898500)
Drottningholm Palace Drottningholm. The royal residence. (75990310)
Riksdag Old Town. The refurbished 19th century parliament building. (100857)
City hall Kungsholmen. An unmistakeable eye catching building by the water. (7859000)
Kulturhus Sergelstorg. A library and the venue of every sort of arts' activity. (141120)
Kaknäs transmitting tower Gärdet. 155m high.

Music, ballet & opera

Berwald Hall Strandvägen. Symphonic & other music. (7841800)
Concert Hall Hötorget. Symphonic & other music. (102110, 244130)
Royal Opera Gustaf Adolfs Torg. International opera repertoire. Royal Ballet Company. (248240)

Literature & the theatre

Drottningholm Theatre Drottningholm. Built 1760s. Lively summer season. (7590406)
Royal Dramatic Theatre Nybroplan. Productions mostly in Swedish. (670680)
Strindberg Museum Drottninggatan. His home for the last four years of his life. (113789).

Life & other sciences

Biology Museum Djurgården. Northern flora & fauna, &

panoramic paintings by Liljefors. The museum's content and form are said to have inspired respectively the American Natural History Museum and the Guggenheim Museum in New York. (611383)
Natural History Museum Frescati. Zoology, mineralogy, fossils, & some moon rock. (150240)
Skansen Djurgården. Zoological gardens. (603000)

The arts

Painting and sculpture
Liljevalch Gallery Djurgården. Exhibitions. (144635)
Millesgården Lidingö. Permanent exhibition of Milles' sculptural work. (7315060)
Modern Museum Skeppsholmen. 20th century art & exhibitions. (244200)
National Museum Blasieholmen. Permanent exhibition of great masters' paintings & sculpture, 16th to 20th centuries. (244200)
Thielska Gallery Djurgården. Permanent exhibition of late 19th/early 20th century art. (625884)
Waldemarsudde Djurgården. Prince Eugen (1865–1947) lived here. The house contains his and many contemporary painters' work. (621833)

History

Hallwylska Mansion Hamngatan. A late-19th century house with its furnishings intact. Guided tours only. (102166)
History Museum Narvavägen. Human life from prehistory to the Middle Ages. (7839400)
Nordiska Museet Djurgården. Life in Sweden since the late Middle Ages. (224120)
Skansen Djurgården. Traditional farm & other buildings in wood from all parts of Sweden. (630500)
Wasa Museum Djurgården. The world-famous 17th century warship: launched & sank 1628, recovered 1961. (223980)

142

Getting about

Fun & games, sport & exercise Funfair

Gröna Lund Djurgården. All the fun of the fair, including openair concerts, restaurants. Open all summer.

Sports arenas

Johanneshov Ice Rink (Johanneshov)
Råsunda Stadium (Solna). Football.
Solvalla Track (Bromma). Trotting.
Stadion (Lidingövägen). Athletics.
Stockholm Globe Arena (Johanneshov). Ice rink.
Söder Stadium (Johanneshov).
Täby Track (Täby). Trotting.

Here are some Stockholm telephone numbers from which information can be obtained in English:

Railways:

domestic services	225060
international services	227940
Stockholm region & tunnelbana	236000

Buses:

Stockholm region	236000
Boats: skerries' lines	140830

Air routes:

domestic (Arlanda)	7975050
International (Arlanda)	7803030
Charter (Arlanda)	7976100

Water transport

Especially in summer, boats leave central Stockholm for many destinations on lakes Mälar and Hjälmaren, in the skerries, and on the Swedish Baltic coast; there are also lines to Göteborg and Gotland, and to Finland, Poland and the USSR.
The Lakes to Björkö, Drottningholm, Sigtuna, Skokloster, Strängnäs, Västerås, Uppsala etc. (City Hall quay)
The skerries scores of destinations (from Ström quay, by Grand Hotel, and Nybro quay, opposite the Royal Dramatic Theatre)

Games to play

Golf There are some 20 courses in the region.
Skating Longdistance skating (e.g. on Baltic ice) should be tried only in experienced company.
Squash Courts etc., are listed in the Yellow Pages.
Swimming Apart from the lakes, there are some 30 public out-of-doors and about 20 indoor pools (some in central Stockholm are scarcely heated).
Tennis Courts etc., are listed in the Yellow Pages.

Regular Stockholm events include the following:

March

Boat Show (Älvsjö exhibition centre)

March—April

Liljevalch's art exhibition (Djurgården)

May

Drottningholm Theatre season begins (ends August)
Confidencen, Ulrikadal, season begins (ends August)

June

Skerries' Ferries' Day (old steamers proceed from Strömkajen out to Vaxholm and back)
Stockholm Marathon
Swedish Flag Day & Stockholm's Festival (6 June)
Midsummer festivities (at Skansen & all over Sweden)
Jazz & Blues All-Star Festival (Skeppsholmen)

July

Round Gotland Sailing Race (start & finish Sandhamn)
Bellman Week (events in various parts of Stockholm) Bellman Day 27 July

August

Nordic Music Festival
Riddarfjärd Swimming Event
Swedish-Americans' Day (at Skansen)
Stockholm Jazz Days

September

Sailboats' Day (central Stockholm waters)
Floating Boat Show (Galärvarvet, Djurgården)
Lidingöloppet (cross country running)
Swedish Trotting Championships (Solvalla)

November

Stockholm Open Tennis (Royal Tennis Hall)

December

Christmas markets on Sundays (Skansen; Stortorget, Old Town)
Nobel prize awards (Concert Hall); Nobel Dinner (City Hall) on 10 December
Lucia celebrations (almost everywhere) & Coronation of Lucia of Sweden (Skansen) on or about 13 December
New Year's Eve celebrations: fireworks and Tennyson's Ring Out Wild Bells (at Skansen).

National & other organisations (selection)

Banking, the stock exchange & the professions

Stockholm Stock Exchange, Börshuset, S-11182 Stockholm. 08/143160

Swedish Bankers Association, Regeringsgatan 42, S-10394 Stockholm. 08/243300

Swedish Bar Association, Laboratoriegatan 4, S-10254 Stockholm. 08/245870

Swedish Savings Banks' Association, Drottningsgatan 29, S-10327 Stockholm. 08/572000

Industry, trade & commerce

Association of Swedish Chambers of Commerce and Industry, Västra Trädgårdsgatan 9, S-10322 Stockholm. 08/231200

Federation of Swedish Farmers, Klara Östra Kyrkogatan 12, S-10533 Stockholm. 08/7875000

Federation of Swedish Industries, Storgatan 19, S-11485, Stockholm. 08/7838000

Federation of Swedish Wholesalers and Importers, Grevgatan 34, S-11485 Stockholm. 08/635280

Federation of Commercial Agents of Sweden, Hantverkargatan 46, S-11226 Stockholm. 08/540975

Swedish Employers' Confederation, Blasieholmen 4A, S-10330 Stockholm. 08/7626000

Swedish Franchise Association, Östermalmsgatan 52, S-10041 Stockholm. 08/7230533

Swedish Retail Federation, Kungsgatan 19, S-10561 Stockholm. 08/7915300

Swedish Trade Council, Storgatan 19, S-11485 Stockholm. 08/7838000

Swedish Trade Union Confederation, Barnhusgatan 18, S-10553 Stockholm. 08/7962500.

Learned societies

Karolinska Institute, Solnavägen 1, S-10401 Stockholm. 08/340560

Nobel Foundation, Sturegatan 14, S-10245 Stockholm. 08/630920

Royal Swedish Academy of Engineering Sciences, Grev Turegatan 14, S-10242 Stockholm. 08/220760

Royal Swedish Academy of Sciences, Lilla Frescativägen 4, S-10405 Stockholm. 08/150430

Swedish Academy, Börshuset, Källargränd 4, S-11129 Stockholm. 08/106524

Other

Stockholm Convention Bureau, Drottninggatan 97, S-10239 Stockholm. 08/230990

Stockholm Information Service, Sverigehuset, Kungsträdgården, S-10393 Stockholm. 08/789 20 00

Swedish Institute, Sverigehuset, Kungsträdgården, S-10391 Stockholm. 08/789 20 00

Swedish Tourist Board, Sverigehuset, Kungsträdgården, S-10392 Stockholm. 08/789 20 00

Stockholm's Site & Development Company, Hantverkargatan 5, S-11221 Stockholm. 08/142880

GULLERS STOCKHOLM
© 1988 Gullers Pictorial AB, Stockholm, Sweden

Designed by Lasse Hallbert Photo by Peter Gullers and by Hans Ekestang (81), Emil Gullers (23, 27), Åke Sandin (55), Stockholms Stadsmuseum (20, 21), Joakim Strömholm (23), Bengt Wanzelius (39), Thomas Wingstedt (12, 13, 30, 31, 44, 45, 68, 69, 72, 73, 82, 83, 84, 85, 86, 87, 92, 93, 94, 95, 100, 101, 102, 103) and Bertil Wöllner (44)

Texts in Swedish by Göran Blomé, Ulf Gudmundson, Oscar Hedlund, Tomas Lagerström and Lars Widding

Translated from the Swedish by Jeremy Franks
Biographical notes ©1988 Jeremy Franks

Cover by Lasse Hallbert Photo by Peter Gullers

Endpaper maps ©Expressen, Stockholm
Conceived and planned by Einar Gullers, K.W. Gullers, Marianne Rydkvist and Gunnar Sundelin

Printed in Sweden by Tryckcentra AB, Västerås, 1988

ISBN 91 86440 30 6
92 91 90 89 88 5 4 3 2 1

Brief biographical notes

Jeremy Franks

Hans ALFREDSON (writer, entertainer, film director; b. 1931). One of a pair of volcanically productive figures – the other being Tage DANIELSSON.

Gunnar ASPLUND (architect, 1885-1940). A leading 20th-cent. architect.

Alice BABS: see Alice SJÖBLOM.

Carl Michael BELLMAN (poet and singer; 1740-93). His songs celebrate low life in later 18th-century Stockholm.

Paavo BERGLUND (conductor; b. 1929). Has conducted internationally since the early 1970s.

Jons Jacob BERZELII (Chemist; 1779-1848). Did work of fundamental importance in early chemistry.

Jussi BJÖRLING (singer; 1911-60). Enjoyed a brilliant thirty-year career.

August BLANCHE (writer & politician, 1811-68).

Ferdinand BOBERG (architect; 1860-1946). Stockholm is full of examples of his work.

Sten-Åke CEDERHÖK (actor; b. 1913). An exponent of music-hall style on stage and TV.

Jean CLAESON (revue artist, 1882-1951). In films from 1917-45. Rival to Ernst ROLF from about 1912.

Tage DANIELSSON (writer, entertainer; 1928-85). Besides his partnership with Hasse ALFREDSON, he wrote the lyrics for *The Animals,* an antimilitarist musical fable, for which Lars Johan WERLE wrote the music.

DE LA GARDIE. Marie Sophie (1627-94): m. Gustaf OXENSTIERNA 1643, widowed 1648; successful businesswoman.

Gösta EKMAN (actor, 1890-1938). Perhaps the greatest 20th- cent. actor in Swedish theatre up to the age of TV.

Gösta EKMAN (actor, b. 1939, grandson to the above).

Hagge GEIGERT (revue artist, b. 1925). One of the stars of Göteborg revue.

Karl GERHARD (revue & film artist, 1891-1964). The Noel Coward of Swedish musical revue.

Isaac GRÜNEVALD (painter, 1889-1946). A major and influential artist from his debut in 1909 until his death in a flying accident.

HASSEÅTAGE (see Hasse ALFREDSON & Tage DANIELSSON)

Urban HJÄRNE (polymath; 1641-1724).

Axel Ax:son JOHNSON (industrialist; 1876-1958). Second generation of an industrial /financial family. JOHNSONCONCERNEN Industrial/ maritime group.

KRISTINA (queen of Sweden; b. 1626, reigned 1644-54, d. 1689). Converted to Catholicism; abdicated 1654.

Zara LEANDER (singer, 1907-1981). After great success in Sweden in the 1930s, she chose to pursue her career in Germany during WW2.

Mats LILJEFORS (violinist & conductor, b. 1944). Has conducted internationally for many years.

Lill LINDFORS (revue artist, b. 1940). In revue since 1961.

Carl von LINNÆUS (naturalist, 1707-78). The founder of modern botany.

Elias MARTIN (painter; 1739-1818). Painted many landscapes in watercolour.

Arne MELLNÄS (composer; b. 1933). Principal works include *Nocturnes,* (1980), *Spöket på Canterville* (1980), *L'Infinito* (1982).

Carl MILLES (sculptor, 1875-1955). His home and studio on the outskirts of central Stockholm is now a museum of his work.

Father MOWITZ. One of BELLMAN's characters: a sentimental musician.

Emil NORLANDER (revue artist; d. 1922) Active from the 1890s until his death.

NORDSTJERNEN (industrial group). Part of JOHNSONCONCERNEN.

Kalle NÄMDEMAN (artist). Flourished until about 1900.

OXENSTIERNA. Distinguished Swedish family.

Povel RAMEL (revue artist, b. 1922). Creator of brilliant, crazy (and untranslateable) texts, and music to match.

Ludvig RASMUSSON (writer). Music critic, journalist and author.

Ernst ROLF (revue artist; 1891-1932). A dominating figure in Swedish entertainment circles during the 1920s.

RÖDA RUMMET (novel by Strindberg, published 1879). Strindberg's first major success. Set in a Stockholm world of writers, painters, journalists, 'The Red Room' is lively, satirical, impressionistic. Its title refers to a private room at Bern's, the popular cafe and meeting place in central Stockholm.

Pär RÅDSTRÖM (writer; 1925-63).

During his seventeen-year career he published some ten novels, collections of short stories and the like, and was active on the radio.

Johan Tobias SERGEL (artist, sculptor; 1740-1814). Worked in Stockholm, Paris, Rome. Suffered from periods of melancholy and isolation; 'Sergelstorg' in central Stockholm, which is to commemorate him, all too easily induces these feelings.

Alice SJÖBLOM (singer: b. 1926). A jazz singer of enormous talent, and one of Duke Ellington's favourite voices.

Wilhelm STENHAMMAR (composer, pianist, conductor; 1871-1927). A dominating figure in Swedish musical life throughout his adult life.

Snorri STURLUSON (Icelandic writer; 1179-1241). Of major importance for the earliest history of the North and of its poetry.

August STRINDBERG (writer; 1849-1912). The Collected Edition of his works is expected to run to some 70 volumes.

Evert TAUBE (singer; 1890-1976). The national bard of 20th-cent. Sweden.

Sven-Bertil TAUBE (singer, actor; b. 1934). Son to Evert.

Ivar TENGBOM (architect; 1878-1968). Early 20th-cent. romanticist. Designed Högalid church (1923), Stockholm Concert Hall (1926).

Alfred Lord TENNYSON (poet, 1809-92). 'Ring Out Wild Bells' *(Ring, klockorna, ring)* is traditionally declamed at midnight on.

Ragnar UPPMAN (architect, b. 1929). Major works include airports, extensions at Göteborg University, Electrum Centre, Kista.

Cornelis VREESVIJK (poet & singer; 1937-87) Dutch-born; gifted interpreter of major Swedish works (eg BELLMAN), in addition to his own.

Lars Johan WERLE (composer, b. 1926). Best known for his music to Tage DANIELSSON's *The Animals.*

Ulla WINBLAD. A euphemistic nymph in many songs by BELLMAN.

Sigge WULFF (revue artist). Song idol at Bern's during the 1890s.

YNGLINGASAGA (Icelandic saga). The first part of Snorri STURLUSON's *Heimskringla,* composed about 1200.

Monica Z(etterlund) (actress, b. 1937) Active since the early 1960s.

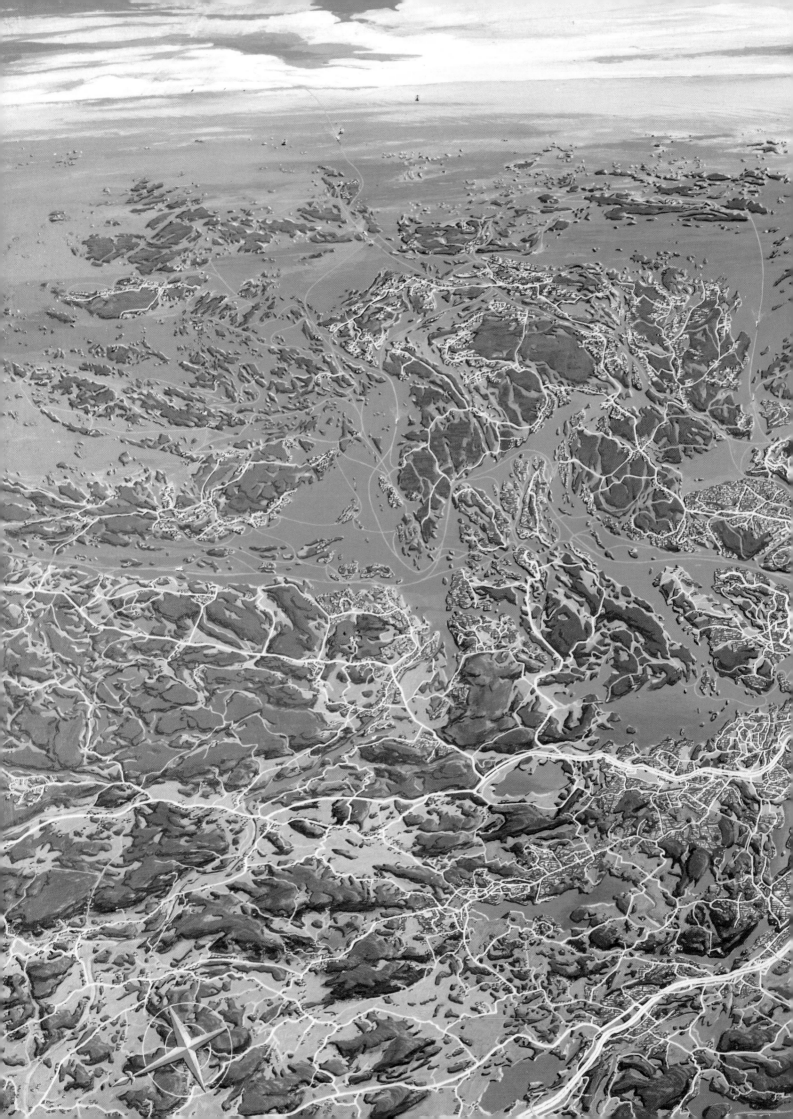